MY BIGGEST PLAYTIME BOOK EVER

First published in the USA 1986
Second impression 1986
Published by Exeter Books
Distributed by Bookthrift
Exeter is a trademark of Bookthrift Marketing Inc.
Bookthrift is the registered trademark of Bookthrift Marketing Inc.
NEW YORK, New York

ISBN 0-671-07933-6

Printed in Italy

MY BIGGEST PLAYTIME BOOK EVER

Exeter Books

NEW YORK

CONTENTS

STORIES AND RHYMES

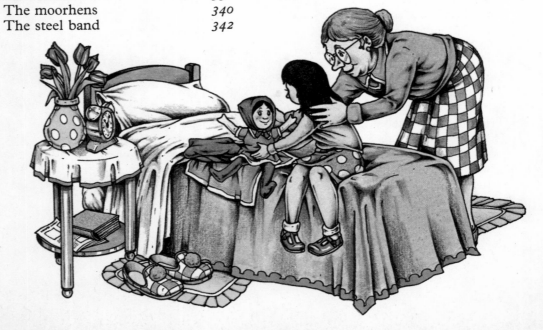

GAMES AND TRICKS

Doreen's quilt

Doreen was a lonely little girl. Her mother and father were busy, famous people, and she could watch them on television most afternoons. She lived in a big, grand house, set in its own gardens.

But there were rooms in the house which she wasn't allowed to use. In these rooms the carpets were white or grey. The walls were pale green or pale blue or pale pink.

The front part of the garden was also forbidden, with its tidy green lawns, and beds of purple and white and yellow flowers.

Doreen ate her meals in the kitchen with Mary the cook, who felt sorry for the lonely little girl. Doreen was allowed to play in the back garden where there was a swing, and a sand pit. But only Mary the cook, or Nellie the maid, ever had time to talk to her and tell her stories.

When Doreen's mother and father were away in another city, and they were often away, Mary had a special way of amusing the little girl.

She would clear the big kitchen table, and on this she would place a linen sheet that was not needed. Then as Nellie the maid cut out scraps of material, Mary and

Doreen would arrange them in patterns on the sheet.

In each corner they had made a cat of black velvet, with white satin whiskers, and blue eyes. In the centre was a huge sun-flower made from two of Doreen's worn-out summer frocks, one golden silk, the other one, green cotton.

When her mother and father were having a party, Doreen would sit in her pretty bedroom, and happily draw with her colouring pencils in her drawing-book.

Nellie would run upstairs with her supper on a tray, and would tell her to be a good little girl, and stay in her room. An hour later Nellie would run upstairs again, to help Doreen undress, and get ready for bed.

When she was by herself, Doreen would think out all the things she wanted on her quilt. A brown dog made from last winter's furry coat. Two pink rabbits made from her too-short dressing-gown.

To please her, Nellie promised to give her her blue satin dance frock, after she had worn it four more times. Doreen spent days thinking out what could be made from a large blue satin frock.

Would it be a sea all round the quilt, with boats on the sea? Or would it be the sky, with white clouds, and sea-gulls? Doreen could not make up her mind. Mary and Nellie would have to decide. What do you think?

At the bazaar

'Jamshed,' his mother said, 'you must take the goat into town to sell. There is no other way for us to get the money we need to pay the rent.' Jamshed's mother was sorry to lose their fine goat, but there was nothing else she could think of to sell.

Jamshed tied a rope around the goat's neck and set off on his long walk. The track was dusty and stony, but at last he reached the busy little town in Pakistan.

'I'll go into the bazaar while I am here,' he thought. Jamshed did not often go to the town, so it was a treat for him to wander round the bazaar, even on such a sad day as this. He loved the sights and sounds of the bazaar and the little stalls selling everything from bright woven carpets to tiny cups of hot, fragrant tea. One man was selling delicious smelling dishes of spicy food which made Jamshed feel hungry.

Still leading the goat through the jostling people he moved on towards a man playing his pipe over a basket of snakes.

Suddenly he heard shouts of 'Stop thief!' A man in blue was running towards Jamshed, pushing his way roughly through the crowds. He kept his hand hidden inside his short coat.

Jamshed stepped back and jerked on the rope round his goat's neck. The rope pulled tight. The man tripped over it and fell sprawling on the ground.

'Well done, boy,' said the stall-keeper who had been chasing the thief. He seized the arm of the man lying on the ground and shook him. 'Give me back the bracelet!' he said sharply.

The man in blue took his hand from his short coat. He held a heavy gold bracelet, skilfully worked in beautiful patterns and studded with precious stones.

'That is the finest piece of jewellery I have for sale,' said the stall-keeper. 'This thief knew which one to steal.'

He turned to Jamshed. 'Come with me. You shall have a reward for your quick action.'

When Jamshed saw the generous reward the stall-keeper had given him he was overjoyed. 'Now I shan't have to sell our goat,' he said. 'My mother will be so pleased when she sees me bringing the goat home again.'

Fun on wheels

The Price family were going to see Granny, who lived a long way away. Before they had driven far down the road, Gerald and Sarah were quarrelling. They quarrelled about who should open the sweet packet. They quarrelled about who sat where, and they quarrelled about who had the bigger apple. Poor Mum and Dad. After another few kilometres Dad stopped the car in a lay-by.

'Can't you two play a game or something?' Mum asked. 'I know. I'll give a small prize to the one who invents the best game, starting now.'

Off they went again, but this time, Gerald and Sarah were very quiet – they were thinking. 'I've got one!' yelled Gerald. 'The first one to see a car number adding up to ten!' Gerald won that game, because he was quicker at adding up than Sarah, but she won the next game because she spotted five different animals on her side of the road before Gerald did.

They counted red cars and blue cars, green cars and yellow cars. They looked for birds and policemen and traffic lights. Soon, Dad was parking the car in front of Granny's house. Mum decided to give Peter and Sarah a prize each. They had both invented some exciting games.

14

Shadows

Malcolm had a lamp shaped like a cottage. The bulb inside shone out through the tiny windows on to the table. If he looked closely at the light, Malcolm could see red and green spots in front of his eyes when he looked away. He could see the shape of the cottage even when he closed his eyes.

He loved making shadows with his hands. If he put his thumbs together and spread his hands out, the shadow on the ceiling looked like a large bird.

When he went walking in the park with his family, he liked to look at everybody's shadow. Daddy's shadow was the longest, Mummy's was smaller and Diana's was smallest of all. Daddy would make Malcolm and Diana laugh by walking with his legs bent and his arms outstretched. It was fun to play jumping on each other's shadows. Malcolm waited until Daddy sat on a park bench and then jumped on his shadow with both feet.

Mummy had shown Malcolm how to draw around shadows and make pictures. She had made a lovely picture of him.

It was one of Malcolm's favourite games and he would play it for hours.

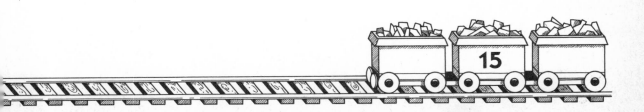

Papier mâché pot

Prepare the papier mâché by tearing newspaper into small strips and making up the wallpaper paste in a shallow bowl. Follow the instructions on the packet when you make up the paste.

2

Cover the outside of the plastic pot with grease.

3

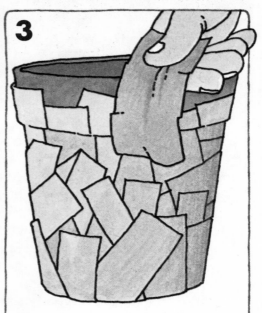

Soak a strip of newspaper in paste then lay it over the pot. Add more and more strips until the pot is covered in a layer of newspaper. When you have finished one layer you must put the pot aside until the newspaper has dried out. Then add another complete layer and let that dry. You must put on six or seven layers and you must let each layer dry before adding the next.

4

↑
LIFT

When the newspaper has really dried out, gently lift the plastic pot out and you will have a papier mâché copy. Now you can paint and decorate this paper pot with poster paints.

Papier mâché pots make nice presents, but remember you can't put anything wet inside them. Put a flower pot or yoghurt pot inside them if you want to grow plants in them.

Chocolate biscuits!

Anne liked going shopping with her mother in the supermarket. She helped to push the trolley, and to get things down off the shelves.

They bought eggs, ham, sausages, cheese, washing-powder, fish-fingers, dog-biscuits, flour, apples, tins of peas, tins of beans, tomato sauce, and bread and butter. Then they came to the shelf that held Anne's favourite food: chocolate biscuits! Her mother always played a game with Anne, pretending to decide *not* to buy biscuits after all, and putting the packet back on the shelf.

Then Anne always said, 'Please, Mum, please! Just this once!'

And her mother said, 'Well, all right . . . Just this once!' Then she smiled and put the packet into the trolley.

One day, when they got home and went into the kitchen, their dog, Happy, jumped up and down as he always did, wagging his tail.

'You certainly live up to your name, Happy,' said Anne's mother, 'but I can't put these things away if you're jumping about all over the place. Anne, will you take Happy out and have a game with him?'

Anne loved playing with Happy, so they went out, and she threw a stick for him, again and again, and he chased after it, barking, and brought it back and put it down at her feet. After twenty minutes, Happy was so tired that he lay down on the ground, panting. Anne went back indoors.

There was no-one in the kitchen. She could hear her mother in the other room, laying the table. Then she saw that the door of one of the cupboards was open. It was the cupboard where her mother kept the biscuits.

'If I just take *one* chocolate biscuit, no-one will notice,'

thought Anne. By standing on tip-toe and stretching her
hands up above her head, she could just reach the right shelf.
She felt for the packet, took out a biscuit, and quickly
popped it in her mouth.

But when she bit on it, she let out a loud yell. It was so
hard, she thought she had nearly broken a tooth. It was dry
too, and tasted horrible. She put her hand to her mouth,
and spat it out, just as her mother came into the kitchen,
saying, 'Whatever's the matter?'

She looked at the bits of biscuit in Anne's hand, and at
her screwed-up face, and started to laugh.

'Well, that just serves you right, Anne,' said her mother,
'for trying to take a biscuit without asking. Do you know
what you took by mistake? One of Happy's dog-biscuits!'

The fish dinner

Crafty Arctic Fox loved playing tricks on the animals at the North Pole.

One day he was sitting fishing by a hole in the ice when Polar Bear lumbered up. 'How's the fishing today?' he asked.

'Very good,' said Arctic Fox showing Polar Bear the fish in his basket. 'But I have to go away for a while. If you'd like to take over, you can keep anything you catch.'

Polar Bear agreed. He loved fish. He waited beside the fishing line, dreaming of a fish dinner. The line jerked.

'My first bite!' Polar Bear pulled in the line. On the end was an old bone. Polar Bear threw it back in. The line

jerked again. This time it was a reindeer antler. 'Someone is playing tricks,' thought Polar Bear.

Then he noticed a mound of snow nearby. He peeped over the top and saw Arctic Fox had dug another ice-hole and had pulled out the end of his fishing line. The crafty fox was tying an old Eskimo mitten to the other end of the fishing line.

Polar Bear jumped over the snow mound and growled angrily. Arctic Fox fled, leaving behind his basket of fish. So Polar Bear had his fish dinner after all.

20

Birthday surprise

Inger and Birgitta lived in a neat white house overlooking the town of Stockholm in Sweden. The two girls were twins and were as alike as two peas in a pod. Each one had long blonde hair tied in plaits with a bright red ribbon. Each wore a pretty white blouse with a blue skirt, and each wore snow white socks.

One day they were sitting in front of their house looking across the town towards the sea. They looked very thoughtful and then all of a sudden they both spoke at once.

'What is going to happen?' they asked. They were so alike they often said the same thing.

'You mean about our birthday party?' asked Inger.

'Yes,' replied Birgitta. 'Do you think they've forgotten? It is tomorrow, after all.' She looked very serious.

The next day was their birthday and after school they came sadly home. No one had said anything all day and they had no presents at all.

'Happy birthday!' There, in front of them, was a table laden with party food and presents and all their friends were there.

The twins laughed. 'Gosh, what a surprise,' they said, both together of course.

Double writing

You will need:
coloured pencils
paper

Have your box of coloured pencils and some paper handy for this trick. It is fun to try when you are sitting quietly on your own or with a friend.

Fasten two coloured pencils together with a rubber band or by tying some string round them. Move one of them down so that the points are not quite level.

Hold the pencils with the longer one on top, so that the points touch the paper at the same time. Now you are ready to do some double writing. You could write your name to start with, then a sentence. See how the colours look, then go on and try some others.

22

Cat and mouse

Play this outside or in a big room or hall. You will need plenty of space. You should have an even number of players – the more the merrier.

Players make a double circle so that there is one person standing behind another one, in pairs. One pair of players becomes the Cat and the Mouse. The spaces between the players are the mouse holes.

The Mouse can go inside the circle but the Cat is not allowed in. The Mouse darts in and out of the circle and the Cat chases him around the outside. The Mouse must not go in and out of the same hole. He must come out at least two holes away from where he went in.

The Mouse can stand in front of a pair of players. The back person of the pair becomes the Mouse and has to run off as quickly as possible. The first Mouse becomes the front person in the pair.

If the Cat is clever enough to catch the Mouse before two minutes are up, they change places. If not, choose a new Cat.

23

Maaui the fisherman

Maaui was such a sickly baby when he was born that his mother thought he was dead and put his body into the sea. Fortunately for him, he was found by the Sky God Rangi who swept him up into the heavens. Rangi grew very fond of the baby boy and treated him like his own son.

When Maaui was nearly grown up Rangi told him about
his family on earth and one day Maaui set off to find them.
After much journeying he discovered his mother and his
brothers. None of them would believe who he was until he
told them how he had been cast into the sea all those years
ago and how Rangi had rescued him. Then they welcomed
him with open arms and kissed and hugged him.

Maaui's brothers soon got rather tired of him, however,
because he was their mother's favourite and she never asked
him to do any work.

One day Maaui decided he must show his brothers that he
wasn't really lazy so he asked if he could go fishing with
them. When they said no, he hid in their canoe, and they
didn't discover him until the boat was far out to sea.

The brothers wanted to row back and leave him behind
but it was too far to go and, besides, Maaui promised he
would find them a good catch. He made them row far
further than they'd ever been before and then cast out his
own magic fishhook into the sea.

There was a great splashing and a huge fish appeared at
the end of Maaui's line, far bigger than any the brothers had
seen before. Maaui told them to hold the fish steady and
wait while he gave thanks to Rangi for such a splendid catch.

But the brothers got impatient and tried to cut the fish up
so they could get it into the boat, which made the giant fish
wriggle fiercely about in the water.

And that is why New Zealand is such a mountainous
country today, for the big fish which Maaui caught is the
North Island, the South Island is the boat they sailed in,
and little Stewart Island, at the southern end of New
Zealand, is nothing but the anchor of their boat. For Rangi,
looking down, saw them all and decided to punish the
jealous brothers and, at the same time, to make a new
country for his beloved Maaui to live in.

The lazy lamb

One spring morning when Robin was walking past Farmer Green's field, he saw that the field was full of sheep.

'All those sheep are ewes,' said Farmer Green. 'Ewes are the mother sheep and soon lots of baby lambs will be born.'

And, sure enough, the next time that Robin went past the field it was full of baby lambs running after their mothers.

Then Robin noticed something far away in the corner of the field. It was a baby lamb, lying down all on its own.

'What a lazy lamb,' thought Robin, as he saw all the other lambs frisking about. And when he met Farmer Green he told him about the lazy lamb.

'A lazy lamb!' said Farmer Green. 'Where is it?' When Robin showed him he said, 'This lamb seems to have lost its mother. We shall have to bottle feed it. Would you like to feed it, Robin?'

'Yes please,' said Robin. So Farmer Green fetched a baby's bottle full of milk and soon the lamb was sucking away happily.

'He was thirsty,' said Robin as the lamb staggered to its feet and began to walk about, 'not lazy!'

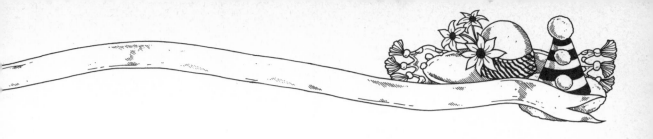

Carnival!

Helmut and Ingrid were very excited. Soon it would be Carnival time. In Germany, where they lived, everyone celebrates the end of the winter. There is dancing and feasting. Brass bands play in the streets and there are processions where everyone wears fancy-dress costumes.

Helmut's mother had made him a teddy-bear costume out of an old fur coat. She had made him a mask with a big smiling mouth and floppy ears.

Ingrid was going dressed as a sunflower. Mother had covered one of Ingrid's dresses with yellow crepe-paper petals. She had made her a bonnet covered with petals, too, and a tiny petal mask.

At last it was the day of the Carnival.

'Oompah, oompah, boom, boom!' Helmut and Ingrid heard the sound of the band approaching.

'Come on,' called Helmut and together they ran and joined the procession. Their friends were already there – one dressed as a mouse, another as a fairy, another as a pirate. Coloured paper streamers and balloons floated through the air. Everyone was singing and dancing.

'Hurrah!' shouted Helmut and Ingrid. 'Hurrah for Carnival!'

Amazing age-finder

You will need

Paper and pencil

This is an amazing mathematical way of discovering someone's age *and* the month that they were born in.

Give your friend a piece of paper and a pencil and ask him:

1. To write down the number of the month that he was born in. (So if he was born in January it would be 1, February would be 2 and so on up to December, which would be 12.)

2. To multiply this number by 2.

3. Then to add 5.

4. Now to multiply the answer by 50.

5. Then to add his age.

6. And now to take away 250.

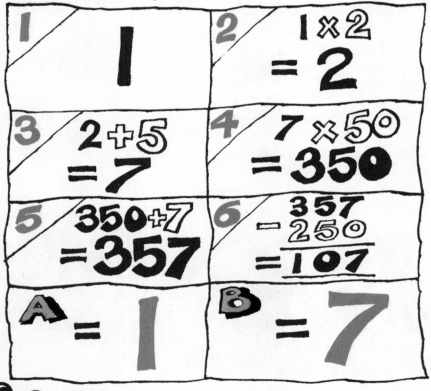

1. 1

2. $1 \times 2 = 2$

3. $2 + 5 = 7$

4. $7 \times 50 = 350$

5. $350 + 7 = 357$

6. $357 - 250 = 107$

A $= 1$

B $= 7$

Now ask him the answer. The last part of the answer tells you his age and the first part tells you the month that he was born in.

If there are two figures the second is his age, the first his birthday month. If there are three figures, the second two are his age and the first his birthday month. And if there are four figures, the second two are his age and the first two are his birthday month.

Left: This chart shows the sums your friend would do if he was born in January and is seven years old.

29

Woolly Rabbit

A tear rolled down Woolly Rabbit's grubby blue cheek.
There he was squashed inside a dark smelly dustbin among
eggshells and baked-bean cans. And all because John had
got too old for him. It wasn't fair.

Rabbit thought back to when he and John had had
adventures together. What fun it had been. And now here he
was in the dustbin. 'I'm just a load of rubbish,' he said
sadly, and another tear rolled down his cheek.

And then he heard the noise he was dreading. The
dustcart was munching up rubbish.

'This is the end of me,' thought Rabbit as he felt the
dustbin being picked up.

The next thing he knew, a big dirty face was smiling down
at him. 'My,' the man was saying. 'If I clean you up,
my daughter Sharon would like you,' and he pulled Woolly
Rabbit out of the bin.

Rabbit rode in the front of the dustcart. He felt very
important sitting there, and very relieved. What a narrow
escape he'd had.

Sharon and Rabbit became great friends. Rabbit was very
happy except for when he saw a dustcart or heard someone
say 'rubbish'. It reminded him of the narrow escape he'd
had and he would nervously twitch his tail.

30

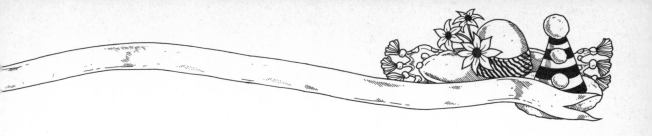

Emily wins the game

It was a wet day and the Miller family decided to have a dressing-up competition. Mum put the dressing-up box in the middle of the room and when she said 'Go!' the four children began rummaging and scrummaging in the box.

Paul pulled out a cowboy suit. The trousers had fringes up the sides, and the waistcoat had a sheriff's badge pinned

on the front. He found the holster and gun buried under some net curtains, and persuaded Patrick to let him have the hat as well.

Patrick took an old white blanket and drew two big round eyes with a black felt tip pen. 'Ooh-ooh-ooh – I'm a ghost,' he said, creeping up behind Tina, who was pretending to be a princess. She had chosen an orange silk dress of Mum's and a beautiful shawl covered with roses.

Emily, who was only four, had to choose from the leftovers at the bottom of the box. On her head she had a battered straw hat, and the rest of her was hidden by Dad's worn-out jacket and a woolly scarf full of holes.

'First prize goes to Emily,' said Mum, 'as the smartest scarecrow in town!' and everybody laughed.

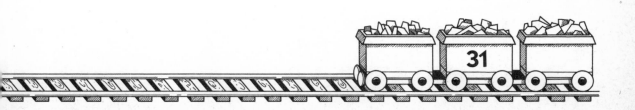

The grey feather

'It's a feather!' Joyce cried.

'But what kind of feather?' Tony asked.

The children looked down from the back door. By their mother's watering can lay a great grey feather.

'It's too big for any bird I know,' Tony said.

'There's another – and another!' Joyce cried. A line of feathers led from the back door across the lawn. The feathers ended in a clump of bushes.

'I love mysteries,' Joyce whispered to Tony. 'Let's see what's there.'

Tony picked up a broom for protection. 'Come on,' he said.

Cautiously the children followed the feathers. Near the bushes were smaller feathers.

'They're fluffy,' Joyce said. 'I'll just look into these bushes and . . .'

Slowly she parted the branches. There was a loud hiss.
Joyce jumped back.

'A snake!' she cried. 'I saw its long neck!'

'I'll look,' Tony said. His voice trembled slightly. One
hand held the broom firmly, the other parted the bushes.

Another loud hiss! Tony let go of the branches quickly.

'It's a great grey goose,' he whispered, 'sitting on a pile
of feathers and fluff.'

'And it comes to the watering can for water,' Joyce smiled.
'Maybe it needs food, too.'

So each day the children placed food by the back door.
And each day they watched as the goose came to eat and
drink.

Then one morning the goose didn't appear. For two days
it didn't come.

But the next morning the goose was back. Only this time
she had a dozen yellow goslings with her.

Paper plate puppet

1

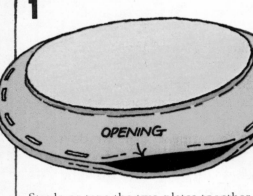

OPENING

Staple or tape the two plates together so that the bottom of both plates is on the outside. Leave a gap big enough to get your hand through.

2

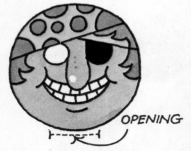

OPENING

Make sure the gap is at the bottom when you paint on a face. Remember you can stick or staple on wool and other scraps of fabric and paper to decorate the puppet.

34

Sock or sleeve puppet

YOU WILL NEED
An old sock or the sleeve cut off an
   old jumper
Scraps of fabric, wool, paper etc.
Non-toxic glue
Scissors

1

If you are using a sock, put your
fingers in the toe and your thumb in
the heel.

2

If you are using a sleeve, tie a knot in
one end. This will be the puppet's
nose.

3

Now you can stick on eyes, ears and
hair. Sock and sleeve puppets are good
for making monsters!

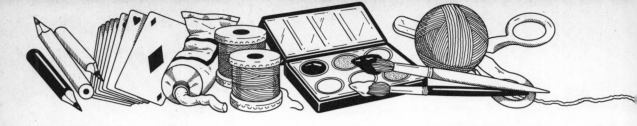

Plastic bottle puppet

YOU WILL NEED
Empty plastic bottle
Sheets of plain paper
Scraps of fabric, wool, card etc.
Scissors
Non-toxic glue
Sticky tape
Your paint box, felt pens or crayons
Pencil

1

Ask a grown up to cut off the top of the bottle.

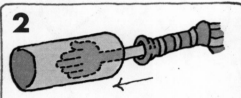

2

Make sure you can get your hand inside the bottle.

3

Cover the plastic bottle in paper. Remember to cover the bottom with a circle of paper as well. Draw round the bottle to get a circle the right size.

Now you can make an animal using the round end of the tube as a face or mouth. Or you can make a person using half of the tube as a face.

Paint on faces and bodies. Use scraps of wool, felt and fur for hair, manes and whiskers. Make arms from pieces of card and stick them on too.

36

Handkerchief parachute

1

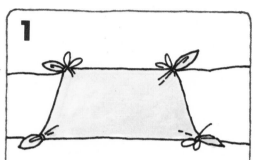

Cut four pieces of string each 30cm (12in) long. Tie one piece of string to each corner of the handkerchief.

2

Tie a piece of string tightly round the middle of the cork.

3

Tie the handkerchief strings to the string around the cork.

4

Draw a parachutist on the paper. Cut him out and tape him to the cork.

Drop your parachute over the banisters and watch it float down.

37

Rose Malairy

Rosa Malairy had one big wish. Her hair was long and black and hung in two thick plaits, but Rosa wished for blonde hair, golden as the sun, yellow as a sunflower.

When anyone said (and this often happened), 'Oh, Rosa, I wish my hair was long and black like yours,' Rosa would reply, 'It's horrid. Black hair is horrid.'

When someone else said, 'What lovely silky hair you have,' Rosa would reply, 'Do you think so? I don't.'

Then one day after school when she reached home, Rosa saw a huge bowl of yellow dye in the kitchen sink. Her mother had been dyeing white curtains yellow and was in the garden hanging them out to dry.

This was Rosa's great chance. She held her head down over the sink and then dipped it again and again into the bowl of yellow dye. 'Now,' she thought, 'I will have golden hair.' She grabbed a kitchen towel and rubbed her hair dry.

When her mother came in from the garden and saw what Rosa had done, she nearly fainted. 'Oh my goodness! Oh my

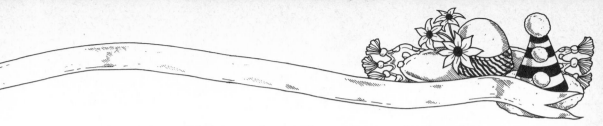

gracious! Rosa Malairy, what will you do next?' she said.

Rosa said, 'I've always wanted yellow hair, and now I've got yellow hair. Does it look nice?'

'It looks awful,' said her mother. 'I'll have to try to wash it out.' But, even as she spoke, she knew that it would be impossible. It was a very strong dye, excellent for making white curtains yellow, but not for hair.

'Go and look at yourself in the mirror,' Rosa's mother said and she spoke in a very faint whispery voice and closed her eyes as she spoke.

So Rosa went to her bedroom and looked in the mirror and when she saw her black and yellow streaky hair, much more of it yellow than black, she knew that she had made a bad, a very bad, mistake.

And next day she was sure that dyeing her pretty black hair yellow was worse than a mistake, for all her school-friends began calling after her, at the tops of their voices:

> 'Rosa Malairy
> looks like a canary.'

Blue or green?

Daniel and Elizabeth watched their dad driving off to work one morning in his new car.

'Isn't it smart!' said Daniel. 'I *do* like Dad's new blue car.'

'It isn't blue!' said his sister, at once. 'It's green!'

The children argued and argued until, at last, Mum said, 'We'll talk to Dad as soon as he comes home again. If he says the car is green, then Elizabeth shall have a little prize for being right. If he says the car is blue, then Daniel shall have a little prize.'

The children waited eagerly for their dad to return and, at last, he arrived home for his tea.

While Dad was eating, Daniel said, 'Dad, our new car is definitely blue, isn't it?'

'No, it isn't, Dad – it's green, isn't it?' interrupted Elizabeth.

As soon as he had finished his meal, Dad brought out the little book that had come with the car.

'There!' said Dad. 'It says on this page – look – the official name of the colour of this model is *turquoise*.'

'Turquoise is a mixture of blue *and* green,' explained Mum. 'That means both of you were right, in a way.'

'But who has the little prize?' asked Daniel.

'You both do,' said Dad. 'The prize shall be a trip out into the country this evening. We'll go for a drive.'

40

Mr Rajpat's buffalo

Indira sat in the courtyard of her home in India pounding meal to make chapattis for the family's dinner. It was very hot and although Indira sat in the shade she soon felt tired. Thump, thump, thump, went the stick in the bowl, grinding the fine powder.

'I wish I had an interesting job like Prem,' she thought. She could see her brother leading the buffalo out to the fields ready to start ploughing. Prem waved to Indira and she left her bowl and went to the fence to watch him.

Suddenly Indira heard her mother calling. She turned and saw that one of Mr Rajpat's buffaloes had broken through the fence and wandered into their courtyard. 'Oh!' cried Indira in dismay. 'He's eating the meal.'

Just then Mr Rajpat arrived to catch his buffalo. It was hard work because the buffalo was enjoying the food so much. Not until every scrap of meal had been eaten did the buffalo let Mr Rajpat lead him away.

'Now you will have to grind some more meal,' said Indira's mother, 'and this time you won't leave it for Mr Rajpat's buffalo, will you?'

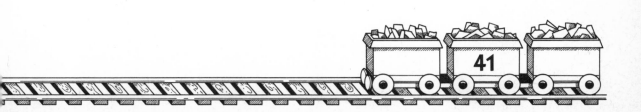

Black magic

This is a 'mind-reading' trick for two people working together. It's good for parties as well as for amazing your friends and family at home and you'll be surprised how long it takes for most people to guess the secret.

One partner goes out of the room and the other asks everyone to name an object in the room. They might choose, for example, the television.

The person outside now comes back in and her partner starts asking her questions like: 'Is it this book?' or, 'Is it my shoe?' The person being questioned will always answer 'No' until, magically, when asked, 'Is it the television?', she will say 'Yes'!

The secret of this trick lies in its name. One of the objects that the questioner suggests should always be something black. (There's always something black in a room, even if it's something quite small, like a watch-strap.) The questioner always suggests a black object *immediately before* suggesting the object actually chosen. So, in this case, when the questioner asks, 'Is it my watch-strap?' (which is black), his partner will know that the next object mentioned will be the right one. So she says 'No' to the watch-strap and 'Yes' to the television!

It's a very simple trick but can be made quite baffling for your audience, particularly if the questioner varies the way in which he asks the questions and uses lots of hand movements like pointing or touching the objects, and if his partner varies the way in which she answers, sometimes answering quickly and sometimes hesitating as if she's thinking hard!

Numbers from nowhere

This is another 'mind-reading' trick but this time you need a secret partner who will pass on the information to you without anyone else realising she's involved.

First you announce that you have special mind-reading powers and that you will prove it by leaving the room while everyone else decides on a number between one and ten. Then you come in and ask all the people in the room to keep thinking very hard of the number.

You move from person to person, putting your hands on the sides of their heads in a way that suggests you are trying to read their minds. Look very thoughtful as if you are concentrating hard.

After touching everyone in the room, announce the number they have all been thinking of and, unless they suspect you of listening at the door, they will all be astounded!

The trick is very simple. When you come to your secret accomplice, put your fingers on either side of his head at his temples. You've probably never noticed this, but if you clench your teeth you can feel the movement in your temples.

So, if the number is 5, for example, your accomplice should clench his teeth firmly, 5 times. Everyone will be so busy looking at you concentrating that they won't notice the slight jaw movements of your accomplice!

Granny's open fire

Gran had an open fire in her house. When the children went for tea she made toast for them. She used the toasting fork, with the sailing ship handle. She fixed the bread on the end, and pushed it close to the fire guard.

'Come on. Get your cushions,' said Gran, and she knelt down in front of the open fire, with the children sitting on cushions either side of her.

'Tell us about pictures in the fire,' said Stella.

'Well, look there,' said Gran. 'Can you see the steps going up to that castle on the hill?' The children looked very carefully, but it was difficult to see what Gran saw.

'I can't see a castle,' said Stella, 'but I can see a great red cave in that bit there.'

'I can see a funny face my side,' said Steven. 'Quick, look before it goes.'

'Oh look,' said Stella. 'His mouth is curling up as if he's smiling.' Then the face collapsed and a huge flame danced up the chimney.

'Gran, I think the toast is burning,' said Steven.

'So it is,' said Gran. 'Never mind, I'll have that piece.'

The holly

It was rather sad in the garden. All the flowers were dead. All the trees had lost their leaves. Everything was brown and ugly.

Lynne looked at her father. 'There's nothing nice here,' she said. 'There are no flowers to pick. There aren't even any pretty coloured leaves left to put in Mummy's vase. They've all fallen off the trees.'

'Look carefully in that corner,' said her father.

Lynne looked and saw something green. She ran over and found a tree which hadn't lost its leaves. It had some bright red berries as well.

'That's pretty,' said Lynne and reached out her hand to touch the tree.

'Careful!' said her father. 'That's holly and the leaves have got lots of prickles.'

'Why haven't the leaves fallen off this tree?' asked Lynne.

'Because holly is an evergreen,' said her father. 'Some trees are called evergreens because their leaves don't all fall off in the autumn. I will pick some holly with berries on for you, so you will have something pretty to put in Mummy's vase after all.'

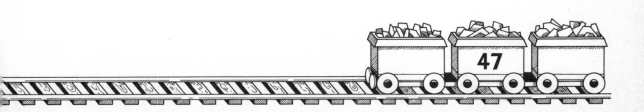

The vain polar bear

Brian the polar bear was very, very vain. While the other bears swam or had races on pieces of ice, Brian would be some distance away admiring his reflection in a hole in the ice.

'My, how handsome I am,' he would say, looking into the water at his bright black eyes and nose, his thick muscular neck and his beautiful soft creamy fur. 'Why, I must be the most handsome bear in the Arctic.'

He spent hours just turning his head this way and that, so he could get a good view of his face from all angles. Once, he tried to see what his back view looked like. But it was a very difficult thing to do, and he nearly slipped into the water!

One day, he was sneaking off to his hole in the ice to admire himself some more, when two of his friends stopped him.

'Come and play with us, Brian,' they said. 'You're always disappearing off on your own. Come and be friendly.'

'Sorry, I've got something else to do,' said Brian.

'Be like that then,' said his friends and they ran off.

Brian couldn't wait to see what he looked like today. Perhaps he'd become even more handsome overnight.

He got to the hole and looked into the water. But he got

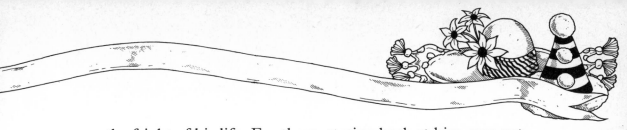

the fright of his life. For there, staring back at him, was not his handsome polar-bear face, but the ugliest, nastiest face he'd ever seen. It had tiny eyes and a funny nose, and, worst of all, instead of fur it had horrible grey wrinkled skin!

Brian let out a roar and ran and ran across the ice to his mother.

'Mother,' Brian bellowed. 'What's happened to my fur? Why have I turned so ugly?'

His mother looked surprised. 'You look just the same to me, Brian,' she said.

Brian told her of the monstrous face he'd seen in the water hole. His mother laughed so much she nearly fell off the piece of ice she was standing on.

'That wasn't you that you were looking at, you silly boy. It was a seal who'd come up for air! It serves you right for being so vain,' and she laughed again.

Brian felt very stupid, but also very relieved. Thank goodness for that. But he never went near that water hole again, just in case. Besides, he soon discovered it was much more fun playing with his friends on the ice, than looking at himself all day!

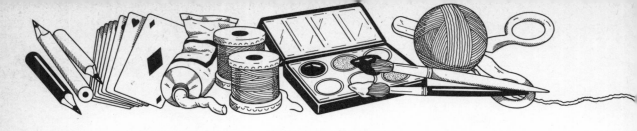

Start a collection

A rainy day is a good time to start a collection – or at least to think about what you could start collecting!

Lots of people collect postcards – from places they've visited or that have been sent to them by friends and relations. Lots more people collect stamps.

But there are plenty of other things you could collect. Here are some ideas to start you off:

Fruit labels – the little labels that are stuck on to oranges, bananas etc. These come from all round the world and are very easy to find.

Matchboxes and cards of matches – you can often get these free from hotels and restaurants.

Buttons – different shapes, sizes and colours.

Pressed flowers – garden flowers and common wild ones.

50

Soap – different shapes, sizes and smells!

Badges – you can wear your collection of these!

Autographs – start with people you know and then see if you can collect some famous ones.

Sweet wrappers – usual and unusual.

Newspaper headlines – history-making or just funny. Keep these in a scrapbook.

Tickets – bus tickets, plane tickets, tickets to places of interest, tickets to the cinema – they all make interesting souvenirs.

It is very important to decide how to keep your collection. It's no fun hidden away in a box or drawer. Try and find a way of displaying your collection in your room. Then you can show it off to your friends.

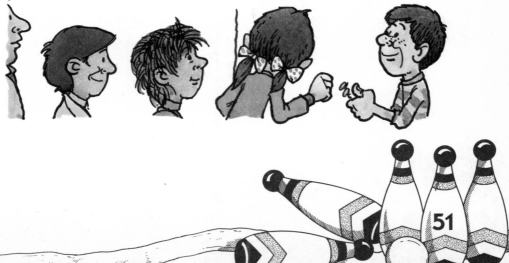

Valentina's ribbon

Valentina, a Russian girl with rosy cheeks, Shamroo, an Indian boy with big dark eyes, and Chiyo, a Japanese boy with a round, jolly face, all lived in a children's home.

It was a very happy place and the children often had parties. In the spring every year they had a party with lots of chocolate Easter eggs to eat.

'I wish I had something special to wear for the spring party,' said Valentina to Shamroo and Chiyo when she saw them all dressed up.

Shamroo had a new blue shirt and Chiyo wore his best leather sandals.

Then she remembered her special treasure. It was a red ribbon she kept in a little box. 'I'll wear my ribbon,' she said, and she tied the ribbon to her long shining hair. But her hair was so shiny and smooth that the ribbon slipped off as soon as the party started.

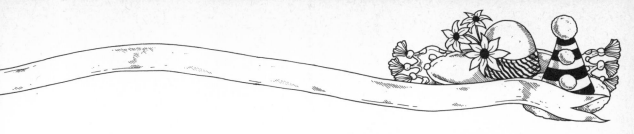

'Don't be sad. We'll find it for you,' said all the other children. And they ran off into the garden to hunt for it.

'Even Pod the puppy is trying to find the ribbon,' laughed Chiyo as Pod sniffed about in the grass wagging his tail.

'Found it!' shouted Shamroo. 'It was near the gate.' And Shamroo had found the ribbon, but oh dear, it was all creased and crumpled now.

'It's not a party ribbon any longer,' said Valentina sadly as she put it in her pocket.

But Valentina had a nice surprise because at the end of the party when everyone was given a chocolate Easter egg – guess what Valentina's egg had tied around it! A beautiful new piece of bright red ribbon.

Then Valentina had a good idea and she said to Pod the puppy, 'Because you tried to find my ribbon for me – I'm going to give *you* a present too.' And she put the old ribbon round Pod's neck. 'And now everyone is ready for springtime,' she said.

Sausage-eating

Walter was very excited. He lived in Munich and today was the first day of *Fasching*. All over Germany people celebrated during *Fasching*, for it was a carnival to mark the end of winter and the coming of spring. And in Munich they had Walter's favourite *Fasching* game – the sausage-eating contest! Walter was a rather greedy boy and loved sausages.

The winner of the competition was the person who ate the most sausages. The sausages were in a long string and two people ate the string, one at each end!

At last it was time for the contest to begin. Walter stood holding one end of the sausage string, glaring at his opponent and waiting for the starting bell to ring.

'Gulp!' Walter swallowed one sausage. 'Gulp!' Another gone. 'Gulp! Gulp! Gulp!'

But then the buttons burst off Walter's suit, one by one. And 'R-r-rip!' The seams on Walter's suit burst apart.

Well, Walter had won. But he was rolling on the ground, he felt so ill. And he had to go on a diet – you can be sure it didn't include sausages!

54

A special day

Just before Christmas, when a thin sprinkling of snow covered the garden, Adam and Penny looked out of the window at the brown sparrows. The sparrows were quarrelling over the scraps Mummy had put on the lawn.

In the kitchen Mummy was busy making mince pies. Adam and Penny decided to help. As they rolled and patted and cut and cooked, Adam asked, 'Mummy, do sparrows know about Christmas?'

Mummy said she didn't think so, and the children said that they wished they could include the sparrows in all their Christmas fun.

Mummy thought, and then she said, 'There is something you could do for the sparrows on Christmas morning.'

Adam and Penny woke up extra early on Christmas Day. Mum got an old branch from the garden and stuck it in a bucket of sand, and Penny and Adam began to thread all kinds of things that sparrows like on to pieces of red wool.

They used currants and apples, peanuts and bacon rinds, and when they'd finished they tied the streamers on to the branch and stood the bucket in the middle of the lawn.

Sparrows came from everywhere and sat on the branch, pulling and pecking. 'Well,' said Mummy, 'I don't know if they understand about Christmas, but you've certainly made it a very special day for the sparrows.'

Heads and bodies

You will need:
paper
pencils

If you feel like drawing some funny pictures, try Heads and Bodies. It is a game for two or more. Cut some long, narrow pieces of paper and find some pencils.

Each person has a piece of paper and draws a head and neck on it. It can be the head of a person or of an animal.

Everyone then folds the paper so that only the bottom of the neck can be seen.

Once everyone has finished, they pass their papers to the player on the left of them.

Each player now draws a body to fit on to the neck. The body should finish at the top of the legs. Papers are folded again and passed on.

This time players add legs and the next time, feet. Then the papers are folded and, for the last time, passed on.

Unfold all the papers. Be ready for a big surprise!

Duel in the West

Two bandits from the Wild West, stand facing each other.
From beneath broad-brimmed cowboy hats dark menacing
looks dart back and forth. Hands open wide over bulging
holsters as the bandits prepare to do battle.

On one side, legs far apart, stands Oklahoma Al, the fastest
man east of the Rocky Mountains. On the other side, legs bent,
arms crooked over his weapons, is California Cal, the deadliest
man west of the Rocky Mountains. A decision has to be
reached: who is the best in the West? Who is the fastest in this
land of the bad men?

Now slowly, now cautiously, the bandits pace towards one
another. One step, two steps, three steps, four, then like
lightning both outlaws go for their holsters.

Out come tin openers in one hand; out come spaghetti tins in
the other. Zip! the tin openers cut open the tins. Gulp! down
go the contents of each super-sized tin.

And in a moment we'll know who is the best, who is the
fastest spaghetti eater in the whole wide West.

Thanksgiving dinner

'Morning, Mrs Jackson,' said Billy to the old lady feeding corn to her turkey.

'Are you looking forward to Thanksgiving, Billy?' she replied.

'Yes, my grandma is coming home to America specially to spend Thanksgiving with us. We're having turkey and cranberry sauce and lots of good things.'

'That'll be nice,' said Mrs Jackson. 'I raised this turkey for my Thanksgiving dinner, but he's much too big for me to eat on my own. Besides I've become fond of him, keeping him in my backyard. I call him George.'

When he got home Billy told his mother: 'Mrs Jackson hasn't any family, and she can't eat George for her dinner, so do you think she could spend Thanksgiving with us?'

'Of course,' said his mother. 'What a good idea.'

So Mrs Jackson didn't spend Thanksgiving on her own after all. Everyone had a delicious dinner; Mrs Jackson and Billy's grandma talked together about the old days; and George stood gobbling in the backyard waiting for his next handful of corn.

59

The ghost train

Robin and George were having a great time at the fair.
They'd been on the helter-skelter and the coconut-shy and
now they were standing by the ghost train, wondering
whether to have a ride.

'I'm not at all scared,' said Robin. 'It'll just be a load of
rubbish. I'm going to have a go.'

'Well, I'm not,' said George.

'Scaredy-cat,' shouted Robin. Feeling just a little nervous,
he paid the man at the door and climbed into the train. It
moved off into the dark tunnel. He heard a witch cackle,
and then a scream. He saw a skeleton, a huge spider with
orange eyes, a large rat, and a green monster. 'It's all
rubbish,' he thought. Then, suddenly, he got a real fright. A
cold hand had slithered round his neck!

'Help!' Robin yelled. 'EEK!' And then the train burst out
of the tunnel into the sunshine. Robin looked round in
terror to see whose hand was round his neck. It was
George's. He must have been sitting in the seat behind
him.

George laughed. 'Serves you right for calling me a
scaredy-cat,' he said. Robin was annoyed that George had
given him such a fright. So, he chased him round the
fairground. But they ended up laughing about it.

60

The grey squirrel

One day last autumn, when Laura and her mother were taking their dog Paddy for a walk in the wood, they saw a grey squirrel. It was sitting under a tree, nibbling at a nut.

'Wuff!' barked Paddy loudly. 'Wuff-wuff!' And he tried to chase the squirrel, but it ran up the tree trunk and hid safely on a branch.

'Naughty Paddy,' said Laura. 'You mustn't frighten the poor squirrel away.'

'It's time for him to collect all the nuts he can find for his winter larder,' said Laura's mother, 'or he won't have anything to eat when the snow comes.'

'Why don't we help the squirrel?' asked Laura. 'We can look for nuts and leave them for him at the bottom of this tree.'

So she and her mother began to search. Paddy thought it was a game and ran backwards and forwards, barking. Soon their pockets were full of nuts and they carried them back to the squirrel's tree.

The little grey squirrel looked down at them from his branch. 'I think he's saying "thank you",' said Laura.

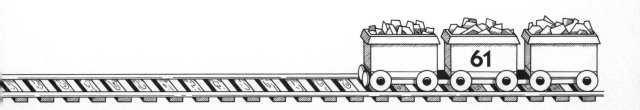

Old Mother Hubbard

Old Mother Hubbard,
    She went to the cupboard,
To fetch her poor dog a bone.
    But when she got there,
The cupboard was bare,
    And so the poor dog had none.

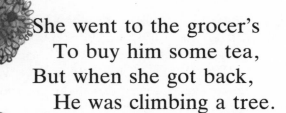

She went to the grocer's
    To buy him some tea,
But when she got back,
    He was climbing a tree.

She went to the hatter's
    To buy him a hat,
But when she got back,
    He was chasing the cat.

She went to the tailor's
  To buy him a coat,
But when she got back,
  He was milking the goat.

She went to the butcher's
  To buy him some meat,
And at last the poor dog
  Got something to eat!

The dame made a curtsey,
  The dog made a bow.
The dame said, 'Your servant,'
  The dog said, 'Bow-wow.'

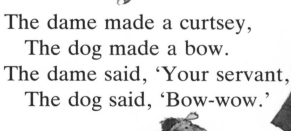

Dots

You will need:
two coloured pencils
paper

Dots is another simple game for two players. To play it, use
two differently coloured pencils and a piece of paper. Make
lines of dots cn the paper. You can have as many as you like.

The first player draws a line between any two dots. The
second player does the same. Play continues like this until
one player draws in the fourth side of a square. That square
now belongs to her and she can put her initial in it.

The winner is the person who completes the most squares.

Hangman

You will need:
a pencil
paper

Hangman is a word game. Two can play.

One player – we shall call him David – thinks of a word. He shows the other player, Jenny, how many letters the word has by marking dashes on the paper. He also draws in a line for the base of the gallows.

Jenny must now try and guess at the letters in the word. If she gets one right, David writes it in wherever it comes in the word. As soon as Jenny suggests a letter that is not in the word, David draws in the first line of the gallows. Jenny has to try and guess the whole word before she is hung. When all the lines have been drawn in, the gallows should look like the ones in the picture.

The peacock

Billy's friend, Karl, was looking very happy. 'Look what I've got,' he said to Billy.

Karl went to his book shelf and he came back with his biggest picture book. There was something peeping from between the pages.

It was a feather! It was the most beautiful feather Billy had ever seen – all blues and greens like a rainbow, all dark and silky with a round coloured spot at the end like a big bird's eye. It was a peacock's feather.

'I keep it on the page where my favourite story is,' said Karl.

'I wish I had a peacock's feather for *my* story-book,' said Billy.

Then, one day Billy's Aunty Babs came for tea and she had a hat on with a feather on it. It was the same as Karl's feather.

'Can I have your peacock's feather to put in my story-book?' said Billy.

'Certainly not!' laughed Aunty Babs. Then she said, 'But if you like peacocks' feathers so much we'll go to the park this afternoon and see the peacock there and we'll ask it to show us its tail.'

So Billy and Aunty Babs walked to the park. Just before they got to the grass where the peacock was, there was a terrible squawking, shrieking noise. 'Peacocks are very noisy birds in spring,' laughed Aunty. Then she pointed to a huge bird with a long drooping tail of feathers that trailed on the floor. The bird was a lovely blue colour with a little feathery crown on its head.

'What a droopy tail,' said Billy. 'Where are all the coloured feathers?'

66

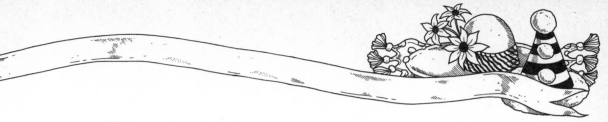

'Wait and see,' said Aunty.

But nothing happened. So Billy said to the park-keeper,
'Where are the peacock's feathers?' and he told him all about
Karl's feather in his picture book.

'Wait and see,' smiled the park-keeper. Then he said,
'Come on, peacock. Show Billy your feathers.'

And suddenly all the peacock's tail feathers rose up in the
air into a huge, brilliant-coloured fan. And the peacock
strutted round showing off his tail.

The park-keeper picked up something from the grass and
gave it to Billy. 'Take it home for your story-book,' he said.

And Billy went home from the park with a peacock's
feather of his very own.

Emma the elephant

Emma the elephant had no friends. She was only a young elephant, but even so, she was much bigger than all the other jungle children. 'You're clumsy!' they told her. 'You're too big to play with us.'

Then, one day, it was too hot for *any* of the jungle children to play. 'Let's go to the water-hole and have a drink!' said the lion cub.

So the young friends set off to the water-hole together. They saw that Emma was already there. She was filling her long trunk with water, and giving herself a cool shower-bath.

'What fun!' laughed all the jungle children. 'Will you give us shower-baths, too, Emma?'

Emma was delighted that the jungle children seemed to want her, after all. The children queued up, and Emma gave each one a cool shower-bath. Then they queued up all over again! They had cool showers until it got dark.

'Please will you play with us again tomorrow?' they asked. 'We'll meet you at the water-hole early in the morning.'

Of course, happy Emma said, 'Yes!'

A heap of leaves

One morning, Derek and his friend Jeremy went to play in the park. The park-keeper had been busy sweeping all the fallen leaves together into a big heap, ready for the lorry to take away.

For a while Derek and Jeremy played on the roundabout. Then Derek said, 'Let's go and play in the leaves.'

So they did. First they climbed up on top of the heap and jumped down again. Then they pretended to be aeroplanes, flying round and round and diving into the leaves. And when they were tired of that, they kicked the leaves into the air and threw them at each other.

'What's going on here?' a voice asked suddenly. It was the park-keeper! 'What a mess you've made of my tidy heap,' he told the boys. 'You'd better help me to sweep all these leaves up again before the lorry comes.'

So Derek and Jeremy helped the park-keeper to sweep up. And when the lorry arrived, the keeper let them help to load the leaves on to the back of the lorry.

And then there was just time to put the broom and the rake away in the keeper's shed before they had to go home.

Handkerchief mouse

YOU WILL NEED
A large cloth handkerchief

1

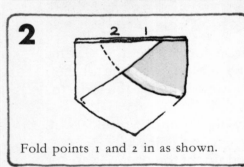

FOLD

Fold the handkerchief in half diagonally.

2

Fold points 1 and 2 in as shown.

3

ROLL DOWN

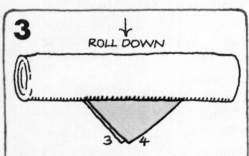

Roll the handkerchief down quite tightly, leaving points 3 and 4 as a small flap.

4

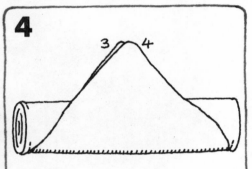

Turn the handkerchief over.

5

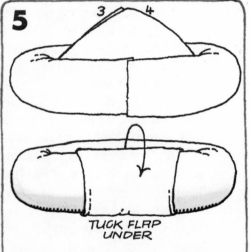

TUCK FLAP UNDER

Fold the ends in and tuck the flap over and under them. Keep rolling the flap in, until you can carefully pull points 1 and 2 out.

6

Tie a knot in one end to give your mouse ears.

Sit the mouse on your hand with your fingers curled underneath the tail. Jerk the mouse up your arm with your fingers. Stop it 'escaping' with your other hand!

Mingo the monkey

The sun blazed down on the jungle. All the animals were sleeping under the trees, except Mingo the monkey who swung along the branches, scaring the birds and annoying the other animals. He dropped out of the trees on top of the tiger, uncoiled the snake, and pulled the lion's tail.

The animals got cross with him, so he went and sat down for a rest, on a rock by the edge of the cool river.

But the rock moved, and started to float away! 'Hey!' squealed Mingo. 'Whatever's happening?'

The rock slowly winked an eye. It was the crocodile! 'I'm taking you for a ride,' smiled the crocodile, swimming a little faster.

Mingo was rather scared. The water rushed past and the crocodile smiled and all his great white crocodile teeth gleamed in the sun.

Then suddenly, the crocodile opened his huge mouth, and, 'Snap!' He shut his mouth again, tossing Mingo into the air.

Mingo fell into the water and when he reached the bank all wet and dripping, he found all the animals sitting there laughing at him.

'That serves you right for teasing us when it is so hot,' they said.

'Well,' said Mingo, 'at least I am nice and cool now!'

Patch's coat

Stephanie lived next door to an old lady called Mrs Scott. Mrs Scott had a dog called Patch and Stephanie often took him for a walk.

One morning Stephanie called at Mrs Scott's door. 'Would Patch like to come out for a walk?' she asked.

'That's very kind of you dear,' said Mrs Scott. 'But I'm afraid it's rather cold out for poor Patch. You see, he is a very old dog and I'm afraid he feels the cold a lot. Perhaps you can take him out when it's warmer.'

Stephanie went home and told her parents about poor Patch.

'I've got an idea,' said her mother. 'I'll knit Patch a coat.' And she knitted a coat out of all her leftover scraps of wool.

The next day Stephanie went to see Mrs Scott again. 'Hello Stephanie,' Mrs Scott said. 'Have you come to take Patch for a walk? I'm afraid it's still too cold for him. He'll have to make do with a run in the garden.'

'I've brought Patch a present,' said Stephanie, and showed Mrs Scott the coat.

'Well,' said Mrs Scott, 'that is kind of you. Now Patch can go out for a walk after all.'

Disappearing Daisy

Dina's doll kept disappearing. 'My doll's gone again,' she said to Mum. 'I put it in my doll's pram. But now there's only Teddy left. Where can it have gone?'

'I haven't seen your doll,' said Mum. 'Are you sure you put it in your doll's pram? It couldn't have gone on its own.'

So Dina went to look for Daisy. She looked in her toy-cupboard. She looked in her bed, and she looked outside.

She even asked the postman because the postman delivered all the letters to the flats and talked to everyone.

'What was she wearing?' asked the postman.

'A long white night-dress,' said Dina. 'She hasn't got any other clothes.'

'I'll keep a look out,' smiled the postman. And away he went.

But when Dina got back to her doll's pram again, *Daisy was there*, sitting next to Teddy.

74

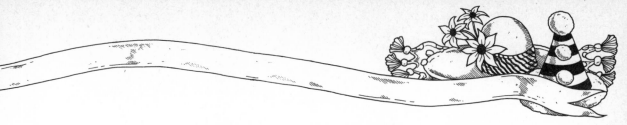

Then the next day it happened again. Daisy went again. 'Do you think she can walk or fly, Mum?' said Dina.

'No,' laughed Mum, 'but it really is a puzzle. We shall just have to watch her very carefully.'

Then Dina had an idea. She took Daisy out of the doll's pram and sat her right in the middle of the kitchen table. 'We'll leave her there, Mum, where we can see her all the time.'

But when Dina and Mum went out of the kitchen, Daisy disappeared *again*.

At tea-time Dina told her gran, who lived with them, all about Daisy disappearing.

Then Gran laughed and said, 'Don't worry – she won't be disappearing any more. Go to my bedroom and look on my bed.'

And there – on Gran's bed – was Daisy. But she wasn't in a white nightie any more. She had all proper clothes on – a pretty blue dress and a knitted pram set with a blue bonnet and blue woolly leggings. She looked beautiful.

'I wanted to give you a nice surprise,' smiled Gran. 'I had to keep taking Daisy away to fit the clothes properly. But now I've finished them!'

Unbreakable balloon

You will need:
a balloon
sticky tape
two hat pins

Everyone will believe in your power as a magician when they see you do this trick. You are going to show your audience that you can stick a pin into a balloon without bursting it.

Prepare your magic balloon before you meet your audience. Blow it up, but not too tight, so that it gives a little when you touch it. Tie a knot in the end. Now cut two squares of clear sticky tape and stick them on to the balloon. Make sure there are no wrinkles.

Blow up another balloon, find a couple of hat pins and present yourself and your equipment to your audience.

Pick out a member of the audience and dare him to stick the hat pins into the balloon which has no tape. There will be a big bang!

Now tell everyone that you are a powerful magician and that you can prove it to them. Hold up the taped balloon and carefully stick a hat pin into each piece of tape. The pins should go through the rubber of the balloon underneath the tape.

Your audience will have their hands over their ears waiting for another big bang. There will not be one. What a clever magician you are! You may now take a bow!

Toothpaste!

Isobel had been sent to her room *again* for 'icing' the wash basin with the toothpaste.

'Why do you keep on doing it?' her mother asked. 'Every morning and evening I find toothpaste crinkled all round the wash basin, over the taps, round the soap, but never on your toothbrush where it's supposed to be!'

'But it's such good fun,' insisted Isobel, 'it just oozes out and lets me make shapes.'

The next morning Isobel went into the bathroom and remembered not to play with the toothpaste. But at bedtime, she made a 'rosebud' on each tap and two 'eyes' on the soap.

Mother was so angry this time that she just put Isobel to bed without saying one word. Then she went downstairs to finish baking her cake.

The following afternoon Isobel asked if she could please have a piece of her mother's cake for her tea.

'Of course, Isobel,' said mother cutting her a slice. Isobel sank her little white teeth into the soft white icing.

Then suddenly she let out a yell. 'It's TOOTHPASTE!'

'And "iced" especially for you,' grinned Mother. 'That should remind you never to treat toothpaste like icing again!'

The snow-creature

One winter morning, a little girl named Lucy woke up to find that everywhere was covered with snow.

'Are you going to build a snowman in the garden?' her mother asked her.

Lucy thought for a moment – and then she had a wonderful idea. 'Not a snow*man*,' she said. 'I think I'll build something different.'

First she made a round snowball, and then she began to roll the snowball through the snow. As it rolled along, it grew bigger and bigger, and heavier and heavier, until Lucy couldn't roll it any further.

'That's the body,' she told herself. Then she made another snowball, but this one was smaller than the first. 'And that's the head,' she told herself.

Then she added two round snow-ears, and a big round snow-nose, and two shiny black pebbles for the eyes, and a thin twig for the mouth. And lastly, she scraped away some of the snow to give the snow-creature two fat paws.

There – it was finished! Lucy was very pleased that her idea had worked so well, and she called her mother to come and see.

What a surprise her mother had! Because do you know what Lucy had built? It wasn't a snow*man*. It was a snow-*bear*!

Sofia and the milk

Sofia's mother lifted the heavy bucket up on to the kitchen table, and measured three jugs full of milk into an open pan on the old black stove.

She wore gold earrings which twinkled like little stars when she moved.

When I grow up, thought Sofia, I shall have earrings like gold stars.

'Watch the milk Sofia, while I let the cow out,' called her mother.

The milk was rising up the sides of the pan when Sofia's mother came back. She took it from the stove and put the pan on the stone floor to cool.

Sofia lived on a tiny Greek island, and every summer the Johnson family from England came for their holiday. It was Sofia's job to take them a pan of milk each morning.

Sofia liked her job. When she had delivered the milk she usually played on the beach with Victoria and Katy Johnson.

'The milk is cool now, Sofia,' said her mother feeling the side of the pan. As she turned her head, Sofia saw that one of her mother's earrings was missing.

'Oh dear, I must have lost it when I took the cow out to the field,' said her mother.

Together they began to look for it – on the kitchen floor, in the milking shed, in the yard where the hens scratched, up the path to the field.

At last Sofia's mother said, 'I don't think we'll find it now, and you must hurry with the milk. Mrs Johnson will be waiting.'

Sofia picked up the pan of milk by its two handles and set off down the stony path towards the beach. She saw

Victoria and Katy waving, and started to run.

But she didn't see a large stone lying on the path. Her foot slipped on it, and she fell, spilling the milk which ran away between the stones.

'Are you hurt?' asked Victoria.

'No,' said Sofia rubbing her knees, 'but what about the milk?'

Victoria wasn't listening. She was poking among the stones. 'I saw something shining,' she said.

She moved a big stone, and underneath it lay the little gold star.

'It's Mother's earring!' said Sofia. 'We looked everywhere for it. It must have fallen into the pan.'

Mrs Johnson came out, and Sofia told her what had happened.

'Don't worry about the milk, Sofia,' said Mrs Johnson, 'and I don't think your mother will be cross, do you?'

Paper bag mask

YOU WILL NEED

A strong paper bag big enough to go over your head

Scraps of paper, cardboard, string etc.

Scissors

Stapler or sticky tape

Your paint box, felt pens or crayons

1

Put the paper bag over your head. Ask a grown up to feel where your eyes, nose and mouth are and to mark them on the outside of the bag.

2

Take the bag off and carefully cut holes where the marks come. Try the mask on again and make sure you can see and breathe properly.

3

Now your mask is ready to decorate. You can add hair made from strips of paper and paint on eyelashes, a nose and lips. Or you can make an animal mask and stick or staple on cardboard ears and string whiskers.

NEVER PUT A PLASTIC BAG OVER YOUR HEAD

82

Tie-on mask

1

Cut out an oval of card large enough to cover your face.

2

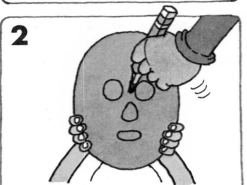

Hold the oval up to your face and ask a grown up to mark where your eyes, nose and mouth are.

3

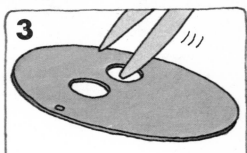

Lay the mask down and cut holes where the marks come. Make two small holes on the edge of the mask just above the eye holes and thread elastic through.

Now you can decorate your mask. Don't forget you can tape or staple on hair, ears etc.

A magic city

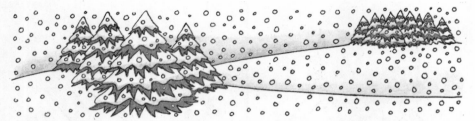

Kaye was staying with her Aunt Vivien and cousin Michael in Montreal for Christmas and New Year. So far, she had had a lovely time. Aunt Vivien and Michael had been so kind that she hardly missed her father and mother back home at all. But one thing she didn't like about Montreal was the weather. She was not used to such bitter, finger-numbing cold. It made her feel almost ill.

One day before Christmas, Aunt Vivien said, 'Come on children. Let's go and get the last of our shopping.'

'Oh no, Auntie,' said Kaye, looking out of the window. 'It's so cold today, I can't bear to go out.'

'We'll go shopping somewhere where you won't have to go out,' said Aunt Vivien. 'You won't even need a hat or gloves.'

Ten minutes later they clambered into Aunt Vivien's car and headed for the inner city. Suddenly, they swooped down an underpass, made a few turns, and stopped in a huge underground car park.

'Where are we?' said Kaye.

'Wait and see,' said Aunt Vivien and Michael.

They stepped into a lift. When the doors opened again they were standing in the middle of a small street. There were little shops on either side, a few pavement cafés, even a fountain, and the whole street was covered with a high roof! Kaye had never been anywhere like it. Other little

streets led off the main one, and everywhere people were shopping and drinking coffee outside the cafés as if it were a hot summer's day.

Aunt Vivien and Michael laughed at Kaye's amazement. 'Come on,' said Michael, 'let's get our shopping done, and then Mum will buy us an ice-cream soda each.'

An hour later they were sitting under a striped umbrella outside a café sipping huge ice-cream sodas. Kaye was still wide-eyed.

'It's only a shopping precinct,' said Michael laughing.

'Not to me,' said Kaye. 'It's like a magic city, where suddenly it's summer in the middle of winter.'

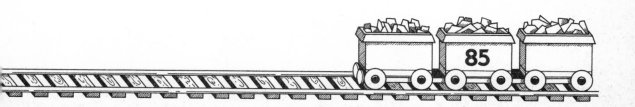

Feeding the ducks

Every day Jean-Pierre and his mother went for a walk in the park in the little Belgian town where they lived. Jean-Pierre liked feeding the ducks and listening to the carillon bells. The bells hung in a tall tower in the middle of the park, and each afternoon a man played tunes on them. He played marches and dances and folksongs and Jean-Pierre marched and danced and sang round the park in time with the music.

When the bells stopped, Jean-Pierre still marched and sang. 'What's that tune you're singing?' asked his mother.

'It's called "Feeding the Ducks",' said Jean-Pierre. 'I made it up myself.' And he marched round the lake singing "Feeding the Ducks" at the top of his voice. 'I wish the man in the carillon would play my tune,' he said.

Very soon it was Jean-Pierre's birthday. 'Can we go to the park?' he asked.

Imagine Jean-Pierre's surprise when the first tune he heard from the carillon was "Feeding the Ducks", his very own tune.

But how did the man in the carillon know, he wondered.

Jean-Pierre saw his mother smile. 'Thank you,' he said, hugging her. 'It's the best birthday present ever!'

An unusual present

'You must write to thank Aunt Eleanor for her Christmas present,' said Roy's mother.

'You mean I've got to thank her for the baby's rattle?' asked Roy. 'Imagine. A baby's rattle! I'm six. How could anyone send a rattle to a six year old? I wish she had sent me something for my train set.'

'Aunt Eleanor is very forgetful,' said his mother. 'She must have got the ages of her nieces and nephews all mixed up. She was kind to send you anything.'

'If she thinks I'm a baby, then she wouldn't expect me to write a letter,' said Roy cleverly. 'Anyway, I haven't got time because I'm going to Peter's fancy dress party this afternoon.'

'You never told me it was fancy dress,' said his mother. 'You'll have to wear ordinary clothes as you have no fancy dress costume.'

'I know,' said Roy suddenly. 'I'll take Aunt Eleanor's rattle and I'll go as a baby.'

The children at the party all laughed when they saw Roy dressed as a baby waving his rattle.

'First prize for the most unusual costume goes to Roy,' said Peter's father, and he gave Roy a lovely red engine to go with his train set.

'I must write and thank Aunt Eleanor for her present,' Roy thought happily.

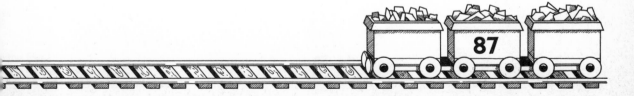

Foxes and hounds

Find a big open space for this game if you can. Divide into two groups. Try and make equal numbers. One group are the foxes and the other group are the hounds.

The foxes run off as fast as they can while the hounds count to ten. The hounds then set out after them.

As soon as a fox is touched by one of the hounds, he becomes a hound and helps hunt down the other foxes.

The hunt goes on until all the foxes have been caught. Divide into different groups the second time round, so that you take turns at being foxes and hounds.

88

Shipwreck

The smaller you are the better, for this game. It should be played with a lot of children out of doors or in a large room. There should be some old furniture or other large objects such as boxes dotted around.

One person is the leader. He calls out 'Shipwreck' and names a piece of furniture or other objects. For example, he could say 'Shipwreck – table' or 'Shipwreck – wooden steps'. All the other players try and climb on to the object. Those who cannot squeeze on, or who fall off, are out of the game. As more and more players are out, the leader names smaller and smaller things to climb on to.

The monkeys

Ajit lived in a very hot sunny place where there are monkeys. Ajit's mum and dad made hats. They made lots and lots of straw hats to keep the sun off people's heads.

One day Dad said to Ajit, 'You must take all our straw hats to the market to sell.' So Ajit took two big baskets of straw hats and fastened them to his little donkey, Dodo, and set off to market. But it was very hot and it was a long way. Ajit began to feel tired and his legs began to ache. Worst of all, he had forgotten to put his very own hat on.

'I wish I had put my hat on,' he said. So he sat down under a shady tree to rest. But there was something Ajit didn't know. He didn't know that the tree was full of cheeky monkeys! They were all sitting amongst the leaves watching him.

Then Ajit had an idea. He took one of the hats out of the baskets and put it on. Then he fell fast asleep.

When he woke up he had a terrible shock! The hat baskets were all empty! 'Where have all the other hats gone?' he cried. Although he hunted everywhere there wasn't a hat to be seen. Someone had stolen them.

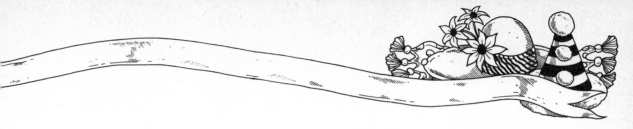

'What shall we do, Dodo?' he said to his donkey. At first, Dodo just blinked, then she shook her head and jerked it up towards the tree. Ajit looked up and saw something strange. It was a monkey sitting amongst the branches – and it had a straw hat on! As he looked more closely he saw more and more monkeys – all wearing *his* hats!

'MY STRAW HATS,' he gasped. 'But how shall I get them back? Those monkeys must have seen me putting on a hat before I went to sleep, and they have copied me!'

He had an idea. He stood under the tree and he took off his own hat and threw it on the floor. Then he waited.

And very soon the monkeys all began to take their hats off and throw them on the floor. Until it was raining hats from the tree!

'They have copied me again,' laughed Ajit. Then he picked up all his straw hats and put them back in the baskets.

'Aren't monkeys funny?' he said to Dodo. And when he got to market he told everyone about the funny monkeys.

Delivering the post

In Canada, the rivers and great lakes are covered with snow and ice almost half the year.

But Carrie-Ann had not played in the snow this winter. She had been ill for a long time.

'Can I get you anything?' her Mummy asked, anxious about the pale, ill face.

Carrie-Ann shook her head, and gazed sadly out towards the forest. In the distance, something was moving. It was the mailman with his dog-team and sledge, coming nearer. He brought them a letter.

'How's our invalid today?' he asked.

'Too pale,' sighed Mummy.

The mailman stared at Carrie-Ann. 'Let her come with me,' he said. 'She could help me by sorting the letters out.'

So Carrie-Ann was wrapped in fur rugs, and placed in the sledge.

The dogs were restless to go, tails wagging. 'Yip! Yip!' called the mailman, and they sped off over the snow.

Carrie-Ann held on tightly at first, feeling scared. Soon, though, she was chatting excitedly, and finding the right letter at each stop.

When home again, the mailman carried her in. He laughed to Mummy, 'I think she's shamming, don't you?'

For Carrie-Ann's eyes were sparkling, and her cheeks the brightest red.

92

Planting bulbs

One autumn morning Matthew's father said to him, 'I'm going to do some gardening today. Would you like to help me?'

'Yes, please,' said Matthew. 'I like gardening. What shall we do?'

'It's time to plant the bulbs, ready for when spring comes,' his father said.

So after breakfast Matthew put on his warm outdoor clothes and went into the garden. The bulbs were lying in a row on the grass. Some were big and brown, and others were small and yellow.

Matthew's father began to dig the holes for the bulbs to go into.

When there were enough holes, Matthew's father showed him how to plant the bulbs. And when Matthew had covered each one with soil, his father told him, 'Now the bulbs will lie in the ground until spring comes.'

'Then what will they do?' asked the little boy.

'Then they'll grow into flowers,' said his father. 'The garden is bare now, but in spring it will be full of colours – red and yellow and blue and white. All from the bulbs we've planted.'

'I'll like that,' said Matthew.

Weight trick

You will need

A sheet of paper
A weight – a large tin of fruit is ideal

Put the paper on a table and place the weight on top of it, in the middle of the sheet.

Ask your friend to remove the paper without touching the weight. Your friend may consider trying to pull the paper very fast from under the weight but it won't work. Eventually he's sure to give up.

Then you show him how it's done! You take the edge of paper nearest you and carefully roll it up. As you keep rolling so the paper will slide out from under the weight, leaving the weight still standing on the table.

(By the way – don't do this trick on a table which will be spoilt if the tin falls over and marks it. Put a thick cloth over the table first or use an old table.)

Invisible writing

You will need

A fountain pen with a clean nib
Half a fresh lemon
A cup
A sheet of writing paper

This is a good way to send extra-specially secret messages – but make sure the person getting them knows how to make the writing appear!

First squeeze the juice from the lemon into the cup. Then dip your pen nib into the lemon juice and use it like ink to write your secret message on the paper.

Your message will be quite invisible until it is made to appear, as if by magic, by holding the paper over a warm radiator or table lamp. It is heat which makes the words appear.

95

Unwin the umbrella

Unwin the big stripy umbrella was a very unusual umbrella.
He hated getting wet! 'It's not fair. I only go outside when it's
raining. Why can't I ever go out when the sun's shining?' he
grumbled. He'd do everything he could to avoid going out in
the rain. He'd brace his spokes so that Mr Wilkes, his owner,
had difficulty in opening him out, and then he'd try and get
hooked up on something so that Mr Wilkes would walk off
without him.

96

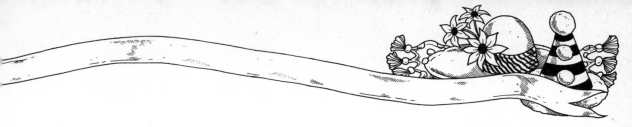

One day he was at the bus-stop with Mr Wilkes in the rain, grumbling as usual. When the bus arrived, Mr Wilkes folded Unwin up and climbed aboard. Unwin sat, feeling chilly and damp, on the seat beside Mr Wilkes. And then, very slowly, he rolled off the seat. Mr Wilkes forgot all about Unwin and got off without him.

'Hurray! I'm free,' thought Unwin. 'No more having to go out in the rain.'

When the bus reached the terminus, Unwin was just hopping off the bus on his handle, when the conductor spotted him. 'You belong in the Lost Property Office until your owner comes and collects you,' he said. The next thing Unwin knew, he was jumbled up with all the other umbrellas, purses, hats and gloves.

Unwin soon grew to like being in the Lost Property Office. He could chat to the other umbrellas and, best of all, he never got wet! His only worry was that Mr Wilkes would come and fetch him. But months went by, and he never came.

One day, a smiling man with a black moustache whose name was Franco came into the office. He said he wanted a big stripy umbrella to go on the table outside his café.

The man in charge looked through the umbrellas and spotted Unwin. 'How about this one?' he said, opening Unwin out to reveal his bright stripes.

'Perfect!' said Franco.

Unwin's heart sunk. He didn't want to sit outside a café all day. He'd get even wetter than he had got with Mr Wilkes. But Franco explained to him that he wanted him to keep not the rain off his customers, but the sun!

It was the ideal job for Unwin. As soon as the sun shone, out came Unwin and the table. Then as soon as it started to rain, Franco took them back inside.

'This is the life,' grinned Unwin as he basked in the sun outside the café. 'I'll never have to get wet again!'

The koala bear

Patti and her twin brother Paul lived in Australia. One day Patti came running to find her brother. 'Paul,' she cried, 'guess what I've found. It's grey and white, with big cheeks, and a nose like a leather button!'

'It sounds like a koala bear,' said Paul. 'Where is it – can I come and see it?'

They both ran up the dusty track, then Patti stopped. 'Under here!' she whispered, and from a bush lifted out a tiny baby koala bear, which snuggled into her arms.

'Poor thing,' said Patti, cuddling him. 'He must be hungry.' So they took the baby koala back to the house to feed him.

They tried him with milk. They tried him with honey. They tempted him with everything they could think of, but the little bear would not eat or drink!

At last Daddy came home, and when they told him about the koala, he laughed, and said, 'Koala bears only eat the leaves of the eucalyptus tree. "Koala" means "no drink" the leaves are food and drink to a koala!'

'Ugh,' said Patti. 'I'm glad I'm not a koala bear!'

The ordinary antelope

Antelope lived in a wildlife park in Kenya. Lots of people on holiday drove through the park and stopped to take photographs of the lions and giraffes and elephants.

'It's not fair,' said Antelope. 'Why doesn't anyone want to take a picture of me?'

'Because you're not interesting like us,' said Giraffe. 'Why, people like to look at me because I'm so tall, and Elephant because he's so big and Lion because he's so handsome. You – well, there's nothing very interesting about an antelope.'

Antelope became very upset. How could he make himself more interesting? He began to leap and dance about in front of the holidaymakers' cars but no one took any notice.

'What on earth are you doing, Antelope?' asked Elephant.

Antelope told him and Elephant chuckled so much his whole body shook. 'You're mad,' he said. 'Do you think it's *nice* to be stared at and pointed at all day? Why, I can't even give my back a quiet scratch without someone taking a photograph.'

Antelope thought about this for a while. Then he said, 'You're right, Elephant. How stupid I've been.' And, giving a leap of joy, Antelope galloped off across the park.

Orange trees

You will need

Some orange pips
A jam-jar
Some earth
Some stones
A plastic bag

Next time you have an orange save the pips and grow an orange tree.

Put some stones in the bottom of a jam-jar and put a little earth or seed compost on top. Push two or three pips into the soil and cover the jar with a plastic bag. Leave it in a warm place and keep it moist.

When the pips sprout, carefully take them out of the jar and plant them in flower-pots. Keep the pots on a sunny windowsill and your orange trees will make lovely house plants.

Cress eggheads

You will need

An eggshell
An eggcup
Some cottonwool
A packet of cress seeds
A felt pen

Save the shell after you've had a boiled egg for breakfast and put some damp cottonwool into it. Sprinkle in some cress seeds and then draw a face on the side of the shell with a felt pen.

Stand the eggshell in an eggcup on a sunny windowsill. Keep the cottonwool damp and within a few days your 'egghead' will have grown some lovely, edible hair!

101

The old lorry

Stan's father worked at a quarry where he drove a huge lorry. One Saturday morning, Stan went with his dad for a ride.

'Wow-ee,' said Stan, when he saw how big the lorry was. 'Do you really drive this, Dad? Its wheels are almost as high as you.'

'Of course,' said Dad, 'but Mr Glover, the man who owns the quarry, says he will have to scrap it soon. He has bought a new lorry.'

Stan climbed in and held on tightly as they drove off. The cab was huge. He loved watching the bulldozers, cranes and lorries.

'It's a smashing quarry, Mr Glover,' said Stan, later. 'And the lorry is so big, it could carry all my friends.'

Mr Glover stood quietly thinking. 'Stan,' he said, 'you have given me a splendid idea. I was going to buy a minibus to take children around the quarry, but I wonder if they would rather ride in this old lorry?'

'Oh yes,' answered Stan. 'It's far better than a plain old bus.'

'In that case,' decided Mr Glover, 'I shall keep this old lorry and give it a coat of paint. Anytime you want a ride Stan, you just ask. Your idea will save me a lot of trouble.'

102

Beards

'Mummy,' Sally whispered, 'That man's got fur on his face.'

Mum burst out laughing. They were in the supermarket and Sally was sitting in the trolley seat.

'That's not fur, silly,' said Mum. 'That's a beard. Let's count how many beards and moustaches we see.

'There's one. Look!' said Sally, and she pointed to a man with a lovely beard. He winked at Sally and Mum said, 'We're counting beards and moustaches.'

'Delighted to oblige I'm sure,' said the man, and he took off his hat and bowed.

Near the meat counter, Mum saw a beard and moustache. 'Number two,' she said. The man turned and glared.

'We're counting beards and moustaches,' said Mum.

'What a silly thing to do,' said the man. Mum pulled a face at Sally.

Sally found the next one. 'That's number three,' she said and pointed to a young man.

'What's number three?' he asked.

'We're counting beards and moustaches,' said Sally shyly.

When they got home, Sally told Dad about their game. 'We didn't count Mr Brown's moustache, because he hasn't got a beard. That would have been cheating.

'Quite right,' said Dad laughing.

Dolls' house

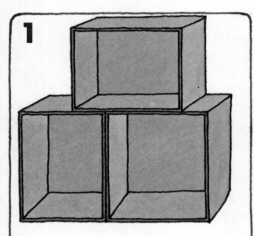

1

Stick the boxes together so the open sides all face the same way.

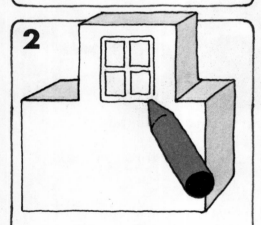

2

Paint the outside of the boxes with white emulsion paint. When this is dry draw windows and other details on the closed ends using your own paints, felt pens or crayons.

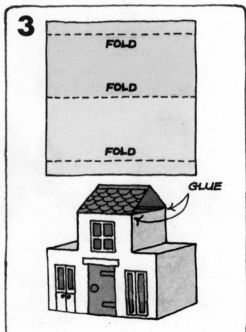

3

FOLD
FOLD
FOLD
GLUE

To make the roof you need a piece of cardboard just over twice the size of the top of your dolls' house. Fold the card down the centre to make a sloping roof. Paint on tiles and stick the roof to the boxes.

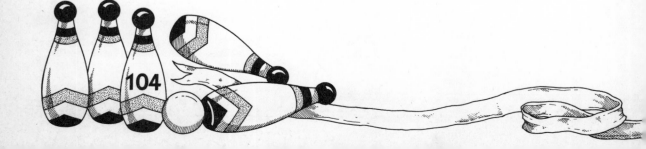

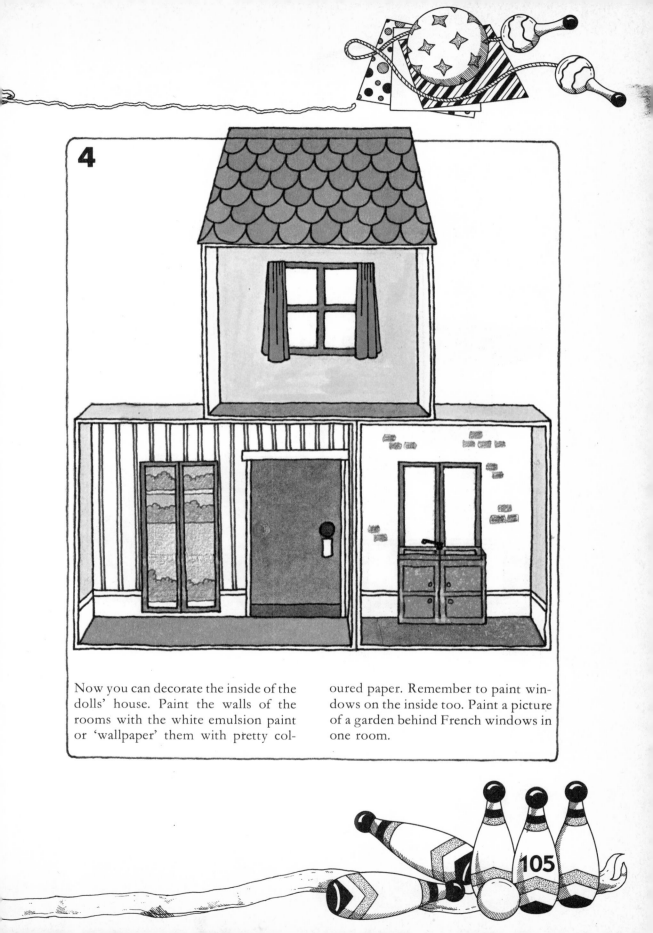

4

Now you can decorate the inside of the dolls' house. Paint the walls of the rooms with the white emulsion paint or 'wallpaper' them with pretty col-oured paper. Remember to paint windows on the inside too. Paint a picture of a garden behind French windows in one room.

Dolls' house furniture

Furnishing your dolls' house is great fun. You can make furniture out of almost anything. Here are some ideas but I expect you can think of lots more.

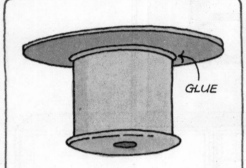

GLUE

Make a table from a square or circle of card stuck on to a cotton reel or cork.

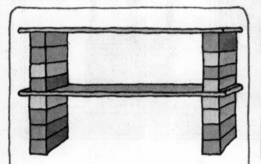

Make shelves from strips of cardboard and toy bricks (or make 'bricks' from Plasticine). Put tiny toys on the shelves as ornaments.

GLUE ON BACK

Make chairs or stools from cotton reels or corks covered in scraps of material. Or cut a cardboard tube into rings and cover them. You can add backs to any of these chairs by glueing on pieces of cardboard.

Make easy chairs and a settee by sticking together matchboxes. Then paint them or cover them with scraps of material.

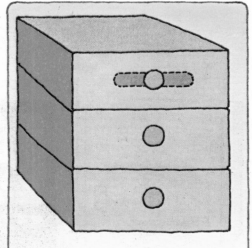

Make a chest of drawers from matchboxes glued together. Make handles by pushing paper fasteners through the front of each drawer.

Make beds from small boxes turned upside down with scraps of material for sheets and blankets.

Small boxes covered in paper and painted make excellent cookers, fridges, televisions, wardrobes etc.

Don't forget to add the finishing touches with carpets, made from pieces of material, pictures cut from old magazines, mirrors made from silver foil stuck on tiny pieces of cardboard and lampshades made from coloured paper. Hang the lampshades from the ceilings by threading cotton through the top of the shade and taping the cotton to the ceiling. Make a lamp by putting a paper shade over a cotton reel or cork.

Castle

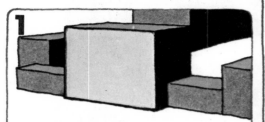

1

Take the large box, turn it upside down and paint it grey all over. Stick the other boxes around it and paint them with grey emulsion paint as well.

YOU WILL NEED
Large cardboard box
3 or 4 smaller boxes
3 or 4 cardboard tubes or plastic bottles
Scraps of coloured paper
Pins
Sticky tape
Non-toxic glue
Grey emulsion paint and a large brush
Your paint box, felt pens or crayons
Cup or glass
Scissors
Pencil

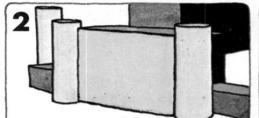

2

Add towers made from plastic bottles or cardboard tubes. Paint them too.

3

Now you can decorate the castle. Use your own paints or crayons to add battlements, windows and doors.

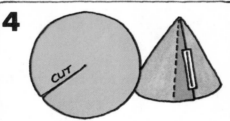

4

CUT

Put paper cones on top of the towers. Make them by drawing round a cup or glass. Cut out the circle and make one cut into the centre. Slip one side of the cut paper under the other and fasten with sticky tape.

Make little paper flags and tape them to pins. Stick the pins in the top of the towers.

If you've got some toy soldiers line them up outside the castle.

In the forest

Kobkua's father worked in the forests of Thailand cutting down trees. Kobkua often watched her father working. She loved to see his elephant lift a heavy tree trunk and trundle it to the river so that it would float down to the sawmill.

Kobkua soon learned the words of command her father used and saw how, as he sat on the elephant's back, he used his knees to tell the elephant what to do.

One night Kobkua's father did not come home. Kobkua went into the forest to look for him, but she found only the elephant. Then she heard a cry for help. She found her father lying beneath a fallen tree.

Kobkua ordered the elephant to kneel. Holding his ear she pulled herself up on his neck. Remembering the words of command, Kobkua made the elephant lift the tree away from her father's leg. Then she rode off to fetch help.

When they heard what had happened the other forest workers ran to carry her father home. His leg was broken, but he was very proud of Kobkua and her skill in handling the elephant. 'My elephant girl,' he said.

The merry moles

One spring day a sad thing happened to Miriam. She was covered in spots and had to stay in bed.

'Cheer up,' said Mum, 'I'll read you a story about three merry moles who made magic castles.'

'Once upon a time,' said Mum, 'there were three merry little moles and they all had pointed noses, thick dark fur coats, and the most amazing creamy pink paws. And because they had such big paws they all dug enormous molehills to live in.

'But one day it rained so much that those merry moles were flooded out and their molehills were completely spoilt.

'"We must find new lands for our castles," said the first mole. "But where can we go? Lots of people don't like our molehills."

'"Let's go to Fairyland, then," said the second mole. And so they did . . .'

'Miriam's gone to Fairyland too. She's fast asleep,' smiled Mum tip-toeing away.

When Miriam woke next morning, she had two nice surprises – her spots had gone and out in the garden something was happening. Molehills were growing up out of the ground before her very eyes.

'Magic molehills!' laughed Miriam. 'The moles have come here instead of Fairyland after all!'

Snowfoot's calf

Every year Inger and her family left their home in the high mountains of Norway and drove their reindeer herd across the snow to the coast for the summer. There the reindeer ate the rich green grass and grew fat ready for the winter.

Inger's father liked the whole family to make the journey together, as the Lapps did in the old days. So Inger and her grandmother sat in an old-fashioned sledge pulled by her father's snow-scooter.

Inger's grandmother often told her stories of the journeys in the old days. Then all the sledges were pulled by reindeer and the journey took much longer.

Soon the herd would reach the coast. They were late this year because one of the snow-scooters had skidded and bumped into a tree. It had taken Inger's father three days to mend it. The snow was becoming softer as the weather grew warmer, and the snow-scooters did not go so fast.

'I hope we have no more hold-ups,' said Inger's father. 'I don't want any reindeer calves born on the way. They can't keep up with the herd.'

'But we couldn't leave a calf behind,' said Inger.

'In the old days, that's what happened,' said her grandmother.

Next morning Inger's father went out early to look at the herd. When he came back, he looked worried.

'Inger,' he said, 'your reindeer, Snowfoot, had a calf in the night. It is very, very small.'

Inger had been given Snowfoot on her last birthday, and she loved the gentle reindeer with her soft, brown hair and dark eyes.

'How many more days to the coast, Father?' she asked.

'Perhaps two, perhaps three,' he said.

112

'Let me go and see the calf,' said Inger.

The new calf lay next to Snowfoot. He was very, very small. 'But he's lovely,' said Inger. 'I shall call him Snowball.'

Her grandmother came up to look. 'He is a fine calf,' she said, 'even if he is small. He'll soon be big enough to keep up with the rest of the herd. Till then he can ride on the sledge with Inger and me.'

'There won't be much room for three of you,' said Inger's father.

'I don't mind,' said Inger, 'and he'll be safe from the wild animals with us.'

So Inger and her grandmother and Snowball were all riding happily together in the sledge, as her father drove the snow-scooter down the track to the summer camp.

Magic ladder

You will need

2 sheets of newspaper
Sticky tape
Scissors

1 Put two sheets of newspaper down on the table, side by side, and stick the two edges together with sticky tape.

STICKY TAPE

2 Now roll the paper up, starting from one side. Fasten the top and bottom of the roll with sticky tape.

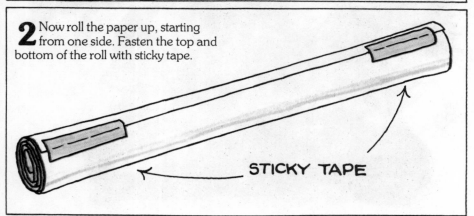

STICKY TAPE

3 Cut a piece out of the side of the roll.

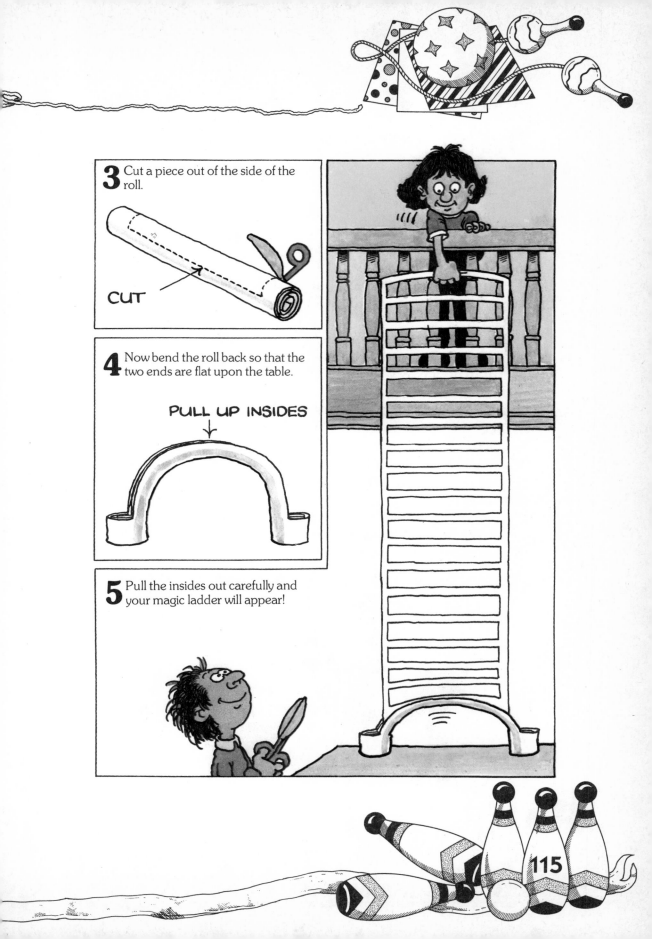

CUT

4 Now bend the roll back so that the two ends are flat upon the table.

PULL UP INSIDES

5 Pull the insides out carefully and your magic ladder will appear!

The hungry reindeer

One winter's day Tarantus the reindeer was feeling very,
very hungry. While he was out in the thick snow trying to
find something to eat he met his brother Rudi. Rudi was
looking fat and happy. He was pulling a sledge across the
snow with a lot of parcels on it.

'Why don't you get a job pulling a sledge, like me?' said
Rudi. 'I always get lots to eat in winter and never feel
hungry.'

But Tarantus shook his head. 'I am a wild reindeer,' he
said. 'I don't want to pull a sledge.'

'You will get very thin, then,' said Rudi. 'The snow has
covered all the moss and lichen and wild bilberries.'

'I know what I will do,' said Tarantus. 'I shall travel to
the big forest and eat conifer buds until the spring comes.'
So Tarantus set off for the forest. It was a long way and he
had to swim across an icy river. 'Oh, I do feel hungry,' he
said, as he travelled across the snow in the darkness.

Tarantus reached the forest at last, and he saw bits of
green showing, as the snow melted.

'Spring at last!' he said as he raced along. 'I shan't need
to pull a sledge like Rudi after all.'

Mark finds a way

One sunny afternoon, Nicola and Mummy were in their garden when suddenly, Mark, who was only four years old, came running across the lawn holding something in his hands. 'I've found a hamster! I've found a hamster!' he cried excitedly.

'What a lovely little thing,' said Nicola. 'I expect it's the baby one that got lost from next door. The girl who lives there said if we find it we can keep it.'

Mummy frowned. 'We can't buy a cage for it until tomorrow and I know we haven't any boxes to keep it in tonight. I think you both should take it back.'

'I'll find somewhere for it,' shouted Mark as he rushed off to his bedroom.

When Nicola and Mummy went to see Mark, he was busily playing with his building bricks.

'Oh Mark, I hope you haven't lost the hamster indoors,' said Mummy worriedly.

'No, it's here,' shouted Mark.

'Where?' asked Nicola. 'I can't see it.'

'It's in here,' Mark said, grinning. And he held up the house made of building bricks. Through the windows they could see the hamster peeping out.

'You are a clever boy,' exclaimed Mummy.' This will be lovely for the hamster to live in tonight, and then we can buy a real cage tomorrow.'

The reed boat

Juan and Manuel were playing by the shore of the great Lake Titicaca in Peru. 'My uncle told me I could use his boat,' said Manuel. 'It's further down the shore.'

The two boys went to find it. 'Is this the right boat?' asked Juan, looking at the broken bundles of reeds which made up the boat. 'It doesn't look safe.'

'Of course it is,' said Manuel, jumping on the boat and pushing off. The boat moved slowly and heavily out into the lake. Then it began to turn in circles. One end was sinking!

Juan ran down the shore towards some fishermen's huts to fetch help. On the way he noticed a new boat tied up. He dragged it into the water and paddled hard towards Manuel. He reached his friend just as one end of the old boat slipped underwater.

'Take hold of the paddle,' he shouted and Manuel jumped across safely.

They reached the shore as Manuel's uncle came up. 'Have you had a good time?' he asked.

'Is this your boat?' gasped Manuel. 'I took the old boat.'

'That old boat was dangerous,' said his uncle. 'They don't last long. I'm glad Juan found my new boat in time.'

The zoo in winter

Johnny was born in January so for his birthday treat he usually went to the circus or to a pantomime but this year he decided to go to the zoo.

It had been snowing all night so that when he arrived at the zoo with his father the snow lay thick and white on the ground, although the sun was shining.

First they visited the polar bears. The polar bears loved the snow. One big, very furry bear kept sliding down a little hill. 'Just like me on my toboggan,' said Johnny.

The huge, fierce Siberian tigers loved the snow too. One of them just lay quietly basking in the sun.

The seals made everyone laugh. Their pond was frozen, and the big floppy animals kept pulling themselves on to the ice to sunbathe, but they were so heavy that the ice cracked and 'splash!' the surprised seals fell in the water!

Johnny felt sorry for the poor chimpanzees. They were all huddled together in a corner and their teeth were chattering. Father said this was just their way of talking but Johnny wasn't sure until one winked at him.

Marbles

You will need:
some marbles
or
very small balls

There are a number of different marble games. This one is for
two players.

One person rolls a marble along the ground. When it stops,
the second player rolls one of her marbles at it and tries to hit
it. If she does hit it, she takes it and adds it to her collection of
marbles while the first player rolls another marble for her to
try to hit. If not, the first player has another go and tries to
hit the second player's marble. The winner is the person
who takes all the opponent's marbles.

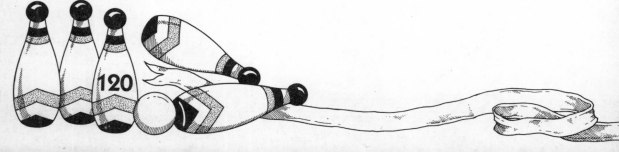

Let's go fishing

You will need:
paper
paper clips
magnets
string
sticks

You do not have to go down to the river to play this game.
You can go fishing in your very own house.

Cut out some fish from pieces of card. Slip a paper clip on
to each one and scatter the shapes on the floor. Now tie a
magnet to a string on a stick and see how many fish shapes
you can pick up. Play it with your friends. The person who
catches the most fish is the winner.

A special present

Duncan had just started school. He had made friends with all the other children in his class and enjoyed all the exciting things there were to do. He had a reading book about a family and their dog, and he had a book for his writing. He liked to count the buttons and the cotton reels, and on Friday afternoons he played in the sand pit, or had tea in the Wendy house.

Duncan especially enjoyed painting, and making models with boxes and glue. He liked making things. One day his teacher, Mrs Matthews, covered one of the tables with a waterproof cloth and asked, 'Who would like to use the clay today?'

Duncan put on an apron and sat down at the table. Mrs Matthews gave him a lump of squashy brown clay. 'Just play with it for a while,' she said, 'and then perhaps you'd like to make something.' The clay was cool and sticky, and it squelched through Duncan's fingers as he rolled and squeezed it. It would be his Mum's birthday soon, and Duncan decided to make her a present.

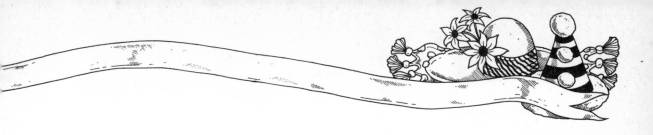

His teacher showed him how to roll the clay into long sausage shapes. Then he patted out a flat circle and wound the sausages round and round the edge of the circle until he had a small dish. Mrs Matthews said it was called a coil pot, and she showed him how to flatten the inside of the pot and make patterns by scratching the clay with a sharp stick.

When the pattern was finished, the little pot had to be baked in a very hot oven called a kiln. Mrs Matthews had to be careful not to drop the pieces of pottery when she took them out the next day, because they were still hot. When it had cooled, Duncan covered his pot with some runny, grey liquid. It was called glaze, and Mrs Matthews said it would make the pot blue and shiny, but first it had to be baked in the kiln again.

When Duncan saw his pot the next day, he could hardly believe his eyes. It was blue and shiny and beautiful, just as Mrs Matthews had promised. She helped him to wrap it up in tissue paper, and he carried it carefully home to give to Mum on her birthday.

Mum was delighted with the pretty dish, and she said it was an extra-special present because Duncan had made it himself.

Port-of-Spain

Many years ago Connie's father was a shop-keeper in Port-of-Spain in Trinidad. Her family had lived in Port-of-Spain since her great-great-great grandfather had been brought over from Africa as a slave.

Connie loved helping in the shop, measuring cottons and silks for crinolines and selling bonnets and parasols. But best of all she liked going with her parents to the harbour each month when tall ships arrived from Europe.

She sat in their little cart and looked after Sugar the pony, while her parents went in search of the goods they had ordered.

Sailors staggered past with bales of shimmering silks and satins, crates of glass and china, boxes of books and iron-bound chests, which she was sure were full of diamonds and rubies. Once she saw a huge piano being carefully lowered on to the quay.

On the way home, her father always gave her a little present 'for looking after Sugar'. It was always a present from Europe. No wonder Connie loved visiting the harbour!

124

The mist monster

It was a very misty morning. The mist was so thick that when Sally looked through her window she couldn't see the garden at all. 'It's like being in the middle of a cloud,' she thought.

After breakfast, she put on her warm anorak and went out to play on the lawn. First of all, she pretended that she was a bird, flying through the clouds. Then she pretended that she was invisible. And then she pretended that she was lost in a strange, misty world.

Suddenly, Sally stopped. There in front of her stood an enormous grey shadow with long bare arms reaching out to grab her! It must be a mist monster!

'What do you want?' the little girl shouted. But the mist monster didn't answer.

Sally felt scared but she went closer. The monster had a long grey body and knobbly, wrinkled skin. And it stood very still.

But then, slowly, something began to move along the monster's shoulder. Sally stared. It was her cat, Clea.

'Clea!' she shouted, and ran to rescue her from the mist monster. And then she saw what the mist monster really was. It was the tree at the bottom of the garden.

Sally began to laugh. Fancy being frightened of a tree!

Plastic bottle skittles

YOU WILL NEED
6 or more plastic bottles
Soft ball
Sheets of plain paper
Sticky tape
Your paint box, felt pens or crayons

1

If you want to make this game very quickly, just tape pieces of paper with different numbers on to the bottles. Then place the bottles in a triangle, stand back and roll the ball to try and knock them down. The one who gets the highest score is the winner.

2

If you've got more time it's fun to decorate the bottles and turn them into people. Cover them in paper then paint on clothes and faces.

Every time you find another empty plastic bottle you can add to your skittle collection.

Cardboard jigsaw

YOU WILL NEED
Sheet of thin card
Picture cut from an old magazine or
    comic
Pencil
Scissors
Non-toxic glue
Heavy books

1

GLUE

Stick the picture to the card taking care to cover the whole of the back of the picture in glue. Press it down firmly and leave to dry under a few heavy books.

2

When the glue is dry, draw a jigsaw pattern on the back of the card. Cut out the pieces.

3

See how long your friends take to put the pieces back together.

Of course you can make a jigsaw from a picture you have painted yourself. Or you can write a secret message on plain card then make the card into a jigsaw. Send the pieces of jigsaw to your friend and see if he or she can puzzle out the message.

127

The present

One day, Mrs Green met John at the shops. 'Would anyone in your house like a goldfish?' she said. 'We're going to Australia, and it's rather a long way for Guinea – our goldfish – to go. If you fetch a jam-jar round to our house, I'll give him to you.'

'I'll give Dad that goldfish as a surprise present,' said John, 'because he always takes me to see the fish in the park.' So he ran home for a jam-jar. But there was only one jam-jar in the house. One very large one – full of strawberry jam.

'I shall just have to eat up the jam very quickly so as to empty the jar for the goldfish,' said John. So he said, 'Please Mum – make me lots of bread and jam for my dinner.'

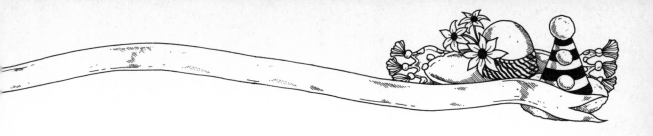

When John had finished he was nearly bursting. 'I must have eaten a *ton* of jam,' he said. But when he looked at the big jam-jar there was still lots left. 'I'll never get through all that,' he gasped.

Mum went to the kitchen to do some baking. 'You can help me to make some jam tarts,' she said.

John was very pleased and he puts lots of jam in the tarts to get the jar empty. But *still* there was a bit left.

Then Mum gave him a bit of pastry and said, 'Make what you like.' And he made *another* big jam tart and emptied the jar.

John took the big clean jar to Mrs Green's for Guinea the goldfish. It was just the right size. So he put a pretty label on and wrote: 'To Dad From John'.

Dad was so pleased that he took John to the shops and bought Guinea a proper fish tank to swim in. So John made *another* present. He stuck pretty coloured paper on the empty jar and gave it to Mum for flowers.

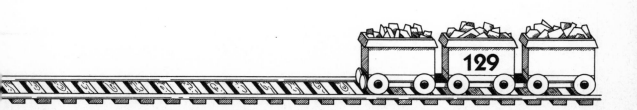

Decorations

Julie and Charlie's father was an artist. One Christmas he took them shopping for decorations for their house. They looked all round a big store, but Julie and Charlie's father thought all the decorations were *very* expensive and he wasn't very rich. 'I know,' he said, 'we'll make our own decorations this year. First we'll visit the heath.'

When they got there they spent an hour picking sprays of gorse and holly and heather, collecting fir cones and even twigs. Then they visited a paint shop, where Father bought lots of little pots of paint.

When they arrived home Father spread newspaper all over the table and began to paint. Julie and Charlie helped him. They painted all the twigs gold and silver, the gorse was painted white and they just blobbed spots of all colours on the heather which looked rather funny but very pretty.

When the children's mother came home from work, she couldn't believe her eyes. 'Goodness, how lovely,' she said.

130

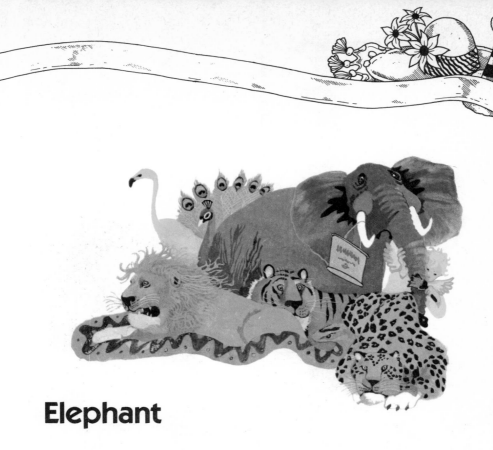

Elephant

Many, many years ago, the elephant was a most unhappy animal. It was about the time God sent his angel to paint all the animals. The elephant was the last to be painted and as he was so large the angel mixed all the left-over paint together and splashed it over the elephant.

When the paint dried out the elephant's skin was a dull grey colour and it was all wrinkled because he had been painted too quickly. 'Bother,' said the elephant. 'Why should I have a grey wrinkled coat, when my brother leopard has a fine spotted fur coat all gold and brown?'

He decided to cheer himself up with a cool sloshy mud bath, and while he was enjoying this mud bath the thought came to him that he couldn't possibly have a lovely mud bath if he had a fine fur coat. Oh, dear no! The fine fur coat would be ruined.

'I think,' said the elephant, 'my skin is just right for me. I'd only spoil a fur coat,' and he blew mud all over himself happily.

131

Dressing up

Dressing-up is always lots of fun and if you haven't already got a collection of dressing-up clothes you might like to start one.

Any old, unwanted clothes will do, the more peculiar the better, although anything, even what used to be your mother's best party dress, can look peculiar when it's four sizes too big and worn with a funny hat and gumboots!

To complete your dressing-up collection you should have a good assortment of hats, shoes and scarves and even old beads and brooches if you can find some.

When you play dressing-up games, don't only think about clothes. You can make masks too. Paper plates make very good masks if you cut holes for the eyes and thread elastic through small holes in the sides to keep the mask on.

Ask your mother if she has any old make-up you can have for your dressing-up collection. You don't have to use it the same way that she does! You can give yourself horrible scars with lipstick, wrinkles with eyebrow pencil and even cover yourself with spots!

132

Decorate your plimsolls

You will need

An old pair of plimsolls
2 or 3 pots of enamel paint
(the sort model-makers use)
A pencil
A paintbrush

Now's your chance to own a really individual pair of shoes – but do ask permission before you begin!

Draw a design out on your plimsolls with a pencil first. You could have stripes, spots, stars, flowers, your initials or just an abstract pattern. Leave some spaces in your design so that the original white colour will be a part of the pattern.

Then start painting, using a fine paintbrush and the enamel paint. Paint carefully so that the results will look really professional.

If you want to use more than one colour paint, then remember to clean your brush thoroughly in between, and wait until the first colour has dried before starting to paint the next one.

Next time you wear your plimsolls you'll be the envy of all your friends!

133

The moon and the stars

One night it was cold and frosty and the sky was very clear. Rosemary could see all the stars and she could see a great big yellow moon floating in the sky as well.

'The moon looks like a great big yellow balloon,' she said to her mother. 'Can I buy a big yellow balloon tomorrow?' she asked. 'Then I can have a moon of my own.'

'Of course,' said Mummy.

So next day when they went out shopping, Rosemary bought a big yellow balloon. When they got home Mummy blew it up.

'I wish I had some stars as well,' said Rosemary.

'I know,' said Mummy, 'you can cut some stars out of my kitchen foil.'

So Rosemary hung the balloon in one corner of her bedroom and stuck some silver stars on the walls.

'Now I've got my own moon and stars,' she said.

134

The fly-away kite

Martin had a new kite. It was a bright yellow one, with a long blue tail, and when Martin flew the kite it soared high up into the air and zig-zagged and swooped and went round and round in circles.

One wild, windy autumn day, Martin went out with his father to fly his new kite. Up it went into the sky, tugging at the string. Martin held on tightly, then, suddenly, he tripped over a tree root and let go of the string. And away went his kite, swooping and circling and zig-zagging over the field. Martin and his father ran after it, but they couldn't catch it.

'Never mind,' said his father, 'I'll buy you another one.'
'But that was my best one,' sobbed Martin.

Sadly, they went home. But when Martin opened the garden gate, he couldn't believe his eyes. Because there, caught in the branches of the tree next door, was his kite!

'Look! It's come home all by itself,' he told his father. 'The wind must have shown it the way.'

135

The sad donkey

Derry was a very sad old donkey. He was sad because he was lonely. Once, when he'd been young, he'd lived at the seaside and had taken children for rides along the sands all summer. Derry had liked that.

He'd liked living in the country, too, at first, when he had been the children's pet and they had played with him every day. But now they were nearly grown-up and weren't often at home and poor Derry spent most of his days alone in the paddock dreaming of the happy times he'd had when he was young.

One cold winter's day, he was standing in a corner of the paddock feeling very lonely and sad when suddenly he pricked up his ears. He could hear children's voices. His master and another man appeared at the gate of the paddock with a whole crowd of children.

His master said, 'That's Derry. He's used to children . . . gentle as a lamb!'

'Oh, isn't he lovely?' the boys and girls said.

The other man smiled and said to the children, 'Well, shall we give Derry a part in our Christmas play?'

'Yes, yes!' they all shouted excitedly and they followed the man through the gate into the paddock and crowded around Derry, patting and stroking him. He wondered what was happening.

After a while they led him round to the big old barn and began to act the play they were rehearsing for Christmas. A little girl they called Mary had to ride on his back and a nice boy they called Joseph had to lead Derry across one end of the barn.

There were more rehearsals during the next two weeks. Derry looked forward to them. All the children talked to

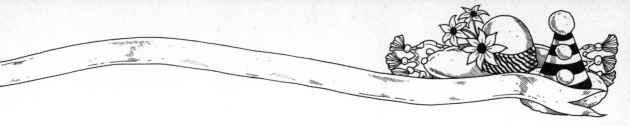

him and stroked him and sometimes they brought him apples. He didn't feel lonely any more.

At last the day came when the children were to perform their Nativity play in the barn for their parents and brothers and sisters and friends.

Derry walked slowly into the barn with the little girl called Mary on his back. Everyone in the audience said, 'Aahhhhhh,' and a little girl shouted excitedly, 'Ooh, look – a *real* donkey!'

Derry felt very proud. While all the children sang 'Away in a Manger' he stood very still, looking into the crib where Mary had put a baby doll she called Jesus.

After that, the children often came to visit Derry in his field, and every year he took part in their Christmas play.

The silver sandals

A pair of silver sandals lay in Tracey's shoe cupboard, feeling very sorry for themselves. 'It really isn't fair!' they sighed. 'The other shoes, boots and slippers in the shoe cupboard are very useful to Tracey, but we don't seem to be any use to her at all.'

The silver sandals knew that on every wet day the red rubber boots were taken out of the cupboard. Tracey wore them when she played in the garden, and they kept her feet dry – even when she went splashing through puddles!

On school days, Tracey took her brown shoes out of the cupboard. They had straps and smart buckles, and they were strong and comfortable.

A pair of canvas play-shoes also lived in the cupboard. They were worn at weekends.

Every morning and every evening, Tracey wore her furry slippers. They were the same colour as her pink dressing-gown, and they kept her feet warm and cosy.

'You are all useful, except us!' sighed the silver sandals, one night.

The rubber boots, the school shoes, the play-shoes and the slippers all thought that the silver sandals were beautiful.

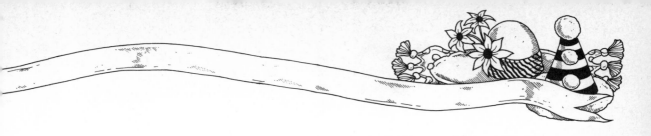

'You are the prettiest of all of us!' they said.

'But we don't want to be just *pretty*,' sighed the silver sandals. 'We want to be useful to Tracey.'

The very next morning, the silver sandals had a surprise. Tracey took them out of the shoe cupboard and polished them until they shone even more brightly than usual.

'I'm going to wear you to a party this afternoon,' said Tracey.

The silver sandals were delighted. 'A party! A party! We're going to a party!' they whispered to one another.

The silver sandals were so pleased and excited to be worn to a party, and they thought it wonderful fun.

Then, on the evening after the party, Tracey told the silver sandals that she was going to wear them to a wedding the very next Saturday – a *wedding*!

'You see,' the red boots said to the silver sandals, that night, in the shoe cupboard, 'you may not go out quite as often as the rest of us, but when you do, you go to very special places!'

Animal costume

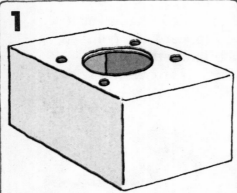

1

Ask a grown up to cut a hole in the middle of the bottom of the box, big enough to fit around your waist. Ask them to make four tiny holes around the centre hole as well.

3

Now you can decide what animal you want to be. When you have decided, paint the box all over in an appropriate colour emulsion paint. Then you can stick on cardboard ears, a string tail etc. and draw on a face using your own paints, felt pens or crayons.

2

Thread cord through the small holes so you have two straps. Try the box on, putting the cord over your shoulders. Make sure the straps are the right length for the box to hang at your waist.

Robot costume

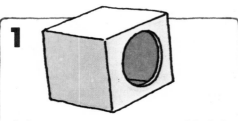

1 Ask a grown up to cut a round hole in the front of the 'head' box.

YOU WILL NEED
One cardboard box big enough to
 go over your head
One cardboard box big enough to
 go over your body
Tin foil or non-toxic silver paint
Cotton reels, bottle tops, corks etc.
Scraps of thin card
Scissors
Non-toxic glue
Felt pens or crayons

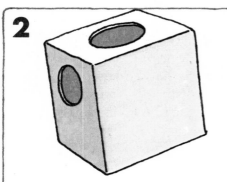

2 And ask them to cut arm holes and a neck hole big enough to put your head through in the 'body' box.

Remember to walk like a robot – with stiff arms and legs – and make robot noises!

3 Now you can paint the boxes with silver paint or cover them in tin foil. Stick on bottle tops and cotton reels and corks covered in tin foil for the knobs. Make cardboard dials and stick them on too.

In hospital

It was Christmas Eve and little Simon was in hospital. He had broken his leg when he fell off a swing in the playground and now he was in plaster up to his knee. He didn't feel ill, but he was very sad when he thought of all the things he would be missing at home on Christmas Day.

That night he couldn't sleep. He tossed and turned in bed until he heard the clock strike twelve. Suddenly, the ward door opened. Simon sat up and so did the other three children in the ward. They hadn't been able to sleep either. In through the door walked Father Christmas carrying an enormous sack. He stopped at each bed and gave each child a pile of presents.

'Now,' said Father Christmas, when he had given out all the presents, 'you must all get off to sleep!'

When Simon woke up on Christmas Day he opened his

142

presents from Father Christmas. He had some felt pens and a pad of paper so that he could draw pictures in bed!

Then Dad and Mum and his sister Becky arrived. They had brought all their presents as well as Simon's so that they could all open them together just like they did at home. The ward was full of families, and all the nurses had tinsel sparkling in their caps.

There was a huge Christmas lunch and Mum had brought lots of dates and nuts and sweets for afterwards. In the afternoon everyone played games and at teatime there was a procession of small children from the local school dressed up as angels, each child carrying a candle. Simon knew that he might have been with them if he hadn't broken his leg and he was sad for a moment, but then he saw lots of his friends waving to him from under their wings and he wasn't sad anymore.

Then everyone grouped round the huge Christmas tree in the ward and sung carols. When Mum kissed Simon goodbye that evening she said, 'I hope it's not been a horrible Christmas, darling.'

'Oh no,' said Simon 'I've had a lovely time, although it will be nice to be at home again next year.'

Sensible clothes

Heather had to go shopping for clothes. She liked clothes and enjoyed going with her mother to the shops.

She had her feet measured in the shoe shop. This was to make sure that her new shoes were the right size. Mum bought her a very sensible pair of brown lace-up shoes for school. They went to the next shop and bought a white school blouse and a grey tunic. A grey cardigan was bought next and a nice navy blue mackintosh.

'Now you need gloves and a hat and a scarf,' said Mum. So, they hurried into the brightly lit shop on the corner of the main street. They found a navy blue hat with a white pom-pom and a pair of gloves and a scarf to match.

Heather looked at herself in the mirror.

'When I grow up,' she thought, 'I shall wear purple feathers, a large cream straw hat with yellow daisies, and a long silver dress, which goes right down to the floor. I'll have a pair of gold slippers with high heels, and a beautiful fan, that has come all the way from China.

'Come along dear, do,' said Mum. 'You're always daydreaming.'

Magnus mouse

Magnus was a little white mouse who belonged to a boy named Danny. He was a very tame little mouse, and Danny often let him out of his cage so that he could run about on the bedroom floor.

One afternoon, when they were playing together, Danny's mother called him downstairs to eat his tea. 'You needn't go back into your cage,' Danny told Magnus. 'Stay here, I won't be long.' And he gave Magnus a piece of cheese to nibble at.

Danny ate his tea quickly. But when he went back up to his bedroom, he couldn't see Magnus anywhere! Where had he gone?

Suddenly, Danny heard a peculiar noise. 'Plink-plonk,' it went. 'Plink-plink-plonk.'

'That's strange,' thought Danny. There it was again – 'plonk-plink.' It sounded just like his toy piano!

Quietly, Danny crept across the bedroom to the toy cupboard. The door was open just a crack, and he peeped inside. And there – was Magnus! He was running up and down the piano keys and having a wonderful time.

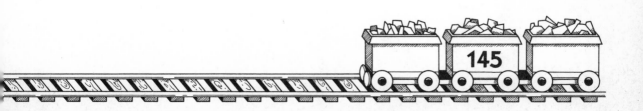

Categories

Everyone has a piece of paper and a pencil and writes down the
left-hand side of the paper a long list of different 'categories': girl's
name, boy's name, animal, vegetable, flower, country, town, food,
bird etc. You can agree exactly how many categories you want.

　　Now choose any letter of the alphabet – perhaps by sticking a pin
into the page of a newspaper. Everyone must try and think of
something beginning with that letter to fill every category on their
list. The winner is the first to finish – or the one with the fewest gaps.

Alphabet game

This is another version of 'Categories' but in this game you write the whole of the alphabet down the left-hand side of your paper and then players take it in turns to choose a category.

   Suppose the first category chosen is 'animals'. Everyone writes down the name of an animal beginning with 'A' then 'B' and so on through the alphabet.

   When you have finished animals, another player chooses a different category. This goes on until everyone has had a chance to pick a category. Compare notes at the end of the game and see who has the fewest gaps.

The nesting box

'How can we make the birds stay in our garden?' Tommy asked his father one spring day. 'They come here to eat the breadcrumbs but then they always fly away.'

'That's because they have nowhere to nest,' said Tommy's father. 'My trees are too little for birds to nest in.'

'Oh dear,' Tommy said, 'I wish we could think of somewhere for them to nest.'

Tommy's father stood and thought for a while. 'I know what we'll do,' he said suddenly. 'We'll build a nesting box!'

Tommy watched as his father made a little house with a wooden roof and a round hole in the front. When it was ready, Tommy's father climbed a ladder and fixed the little nesting box securely on to the wall.

For days and days they watched to see if any birds would go into their new house.

Then one day a little bluetit flew straight into the house and chirruped eagerly to its mate. Then the two bluetits worked busily with bits of moss and odds and ends until their nest was complete.

'Now we have some birds who stay in our garden,' said Tommy.

Blowing bubbles

Angus hated washing his hands, and every time he came in from playing, his mother would say: 'Angus your hands are very dirty. Go and wash them, please.'

One day, Angus's granny was there when he came rushing into the house after playing in the garden.

'Go and wash your hands please, Angus,' his mother said, smiling. 'Granny's brought a lovely chocolate cake for tea. So don't be long.'

Angus looked at his dirty hands and sighed.

'Come on, love,' Granny said. 'I'll show you a game you can play when you wash your hands.'

They went up to the bathroom and Granny filled the washbasin with warm water. Then she took the bar of soap and rubbed and rubbed it into her hands. Very carefully, she made her thumb and finger into a round ring and Angus could see the thin film of soap shining pretty colours in the light. Then he gasped. Granny blew on the soap very gently until it made a huge bubble.

Angus was so excited, he wanted to try it himself. Now he doesn't mind washing his hands at all.

Daniel the dragon

One very sunny day, Daniel the dragon saw some children standing in a long line beside a van.

'Come and join us, Daniel,' they called. 'We're waiting to be served by the ice-cream man.'

'What *is* ice-cream?' Daniel asked.

'It's cold, and sweet and lovely,' said the children. 'You'll like it.'

When Daniel's turn came to be served, he chose a pink ice-cream cornet. A boy called Alexander held the cornet up high, and Daniel stretched down his long neck and licked at the pink ice-cream. 'Delicious!' he said.

'While we eat our ices, Daniel, will you do your best trick for us?' asked Alexander. 'Will you breath smoke rings?'

Now, everyone knows that dragons can breathe smoke and flames, but what Daniel didn't know was that the cold ice-cream had put out his dragon fire! When Daniel tried to breathe smoke, he couldn't even make one tiny ring!

The children were disappointed. 'Perhaps dragons shouldn't eat ice-cream,' said Alexander.

'Oh how sad!' sighed Daniel. 'The ice-cream was so cool and lovely that I wanted to have one on every summer day.'

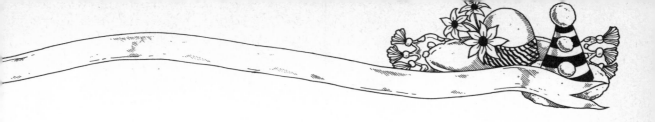

Daniel looked so upset that the ice-cream man left his van for a while and came to talk to the dragon.

'I have an idea, Daniel,' he said. 'I'll make you some special ice-creams, and I'll flavour them with hot, spicy things like mustard, and pepper and ginger. Hot spicy things like that will keep your fire going, I'm sure.'

The next day, the ice-cream man returned, and Daniel chose three of his special ices. One was mustard flavoured, one ginger and one pepper.

'How horrid!' said Alexander.

He held up the cornets, and Daniel licked off the three ice-creams. 'They're delicious,' he said. 'They are lovely and cold, and yet they taste hot. They make me feel cool, but my tummy feels nice and fiery.'

When Daniel had finished his special ice-creams, he blew the best smoke rings that he had ever blown.

Cheating

You will need:
one or more packs of cards

This game is a good one for parties because it can be played by any number of people. You can use up to four packs of cards.

Shuffle the packs together. If necessary remove a few cards so that everyone starts off with the same number of cards. Deal them out.

The player on the left of the dealer begins. She places a card face down in the centre of the table, saying the number of the card. For example she might say it is a five. The next player must call out six and place a card on top, continuing round the table up to King, then Ace then two, then three, and so on.

The trick of the game is that the player might not say the true number of the card that she is playing. So when a player has said a number, she can be accused of cheating by any of the other players. If she is found to be cheating she has to pick up all the cards on the table. But if she is wrongly accused, the accuser must take all the cards into his hand.

The game is started again by the player on the left of the accuser. He plays a card to the centre of the table and announces it.

The person who is the first to get rid of all his cards is the winner.

152

There was a piper

There was a piper had a cow
And had no hay to give her.
He played a tune upon his pipes,
'Consider, old cow, consider!'

The old cow considered well
And promised her master money,
Only to play that other tune,
'Corn-riggs are bonny.'

Polly put the kettle on

Polly, put the kettle on,
Polly, put the kettle on,
Polly, put the kettle on,
We'll all have tea.

Sally, take it off again,
Sally, take it off again,
Sally, take it off again,
They've all gone away.

154

Betty Botter

Betty Botter bought some butter,
  'But,' she said, 'the butter's bitter!
If I put it in my batter,
  It will make my batter bitter.
But a bit of better butter
  Will make my batter better!'

So she bought a bit of butter,
  Better than the bitter butter.
And she put it in her batter,
  And the batter was not bitter.
So 'twas better Betty Botter
  Bought some better butter.

The witch's trick

'You wicked, wicked boy,' cackled the ugly witch. 'You used your sister's bicycle without her permission and now it's got a puncture. I'm going to punish you in a horrible way.'

At first, David thought he was having a nightmare. But no, he was definitely awake and there was definitely a witch bending over his bed. He started to shake.

'Now, what spell shall I cast on you?' said the witch. 'Shall I turn you into a toad? Or shall I boil you up and eat you for breakfast?' and she cackled, showing her black teeth.

'No, please don't,' shouted David, white with fear.

Then the witch laughed, an ordinary laugh this time, and she took off her hat. It was his sister Jane! 'I hope I didn't frighten you too much,' she said, 'but it serves you right for using my bike.'

For her disguise, Jane used black card for her hat, white powder on her face, black wax crayon to blacken her teeth. Her cloak was a black curtain. Her hands were rubber gloves with long pieces of black card stuck on to the ends of the fingers to look like fingernails.

If you dress up as a witch, make sure you don't frighten people too much!

Help for Louise

When Louise arrived on the beach with her parents, the first thing she wanted to do was to build a sandcastle with her new bucket and spade. She dug and dug and soon she had a big pile of sand. Carefully, she smoothed down the sides and put paper flags on the top. She thought it looked wonderful. Suddenly, a big black dog bounded up. 'Woof! Woof!' he barked.

'Careful,' warned Louise, but it was too late. The big black dog had jumped right on top of her castle and knocked it down.

'Oh no!' said Louise. 'Just look what you've done!'

'Woof,' said the dog sadly.

'You didn't mean to, did you?' said Louise. 'Oh well, I'll just have to build another castle.'

She started digging while the dog sat and watched. Then he started digging, too. Soon, the big black dog had dug a very big hole, and there was a pile of sand all ready to make into a castle. The dog wagged his tail proudly.

Louise was delighted. 'What a clever dog,' she said to him. 'When I've finished, this castle will be even bigger than it was before.'

'Woof!' agreed the dog, and he sat down to guard his castle.

The red socks

The Threadgold family had been invited to their cousin's wedding. Johnathan, who was the youngest member of the family, immediately decided that he wanted to wear his new red socks for the occasion because they were his favourite pair.

'You can't wear red socks,' his sister Judith exclaimed. 'Not to a posh wedding. You'll look like a footballer.'

'He's not wearing his red socks,' Mother said sternly. 'He'll wear what I say he'll wear and that's that!'

'What colour can I wear then?' Johnathan mumbled under his breath.

'White,' said his father.

'*White?*' shouted Johnathan. 'White isn't a colour. I hate white, my legs are white, in fact all of me is white and, besides, Judith always wears white socks and I don't want to wear the same as her . . . I don't want to.'

'That's enough, thank you Johnathan,' said his mother firmly.

Johnathan didn't mention the matter again until a few

days before the wedding when he managed to persuade Judith to agree to smuggle out his favourite red socks under her hat!

The big day arrived and Johnathan happily went to the church in his white socks.

While the choir and congregation sang, Johnathan quietly removed one white sock, and then another white sock and stuffed them behind a radiator!

Getting the red socks out from under Judith's hat was a bit more difficult, but they managed it and when everyone got down to pray Johnathan popped them on. PHEW!

With their heads in the air and staring straight ahead the children followed the congregation, who followed the bride and groom, into the sunshine outside.

'Johnathan!' It was his mother's voice. 'How *could* you! After all I said. Where are your proper wedding socks? Where . . .' She stopped as the photographer pointed his camera at them all.

'Smile everybody, please,' shouted the photographer. Just at that moment the bridegroom yelled 'SNAP!', lifted up the legs of his trousers and exposed a pair of the brightest red socks you have ever seen.

What a picture!

Puppet theatre

YOU WILL NEED
A large cardboard box
Emulsion paint and large brush
Scissors

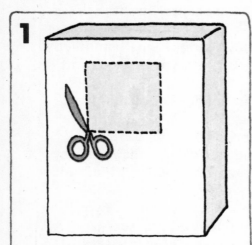

1

Ask a grown up to cut a square hole in the box, as shown.

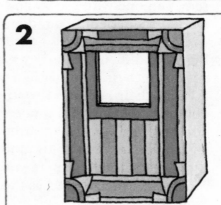

2

Paint the outside of your theatre, get inside with your puppets, and you are ready to give a puppet show.

3

If you like you can make your box into a television instead and make up your own programmes.

Newspaper hat

This is a very easy hat to make. If you make it and like it perhaps you could find a piece of plain paper big enough to make it from as you can't paint or colour newspaper very easily.

YOU WILL NEED
Sheet of newspaper
Sticky tape
Strip of tissue paper
Scissors

1

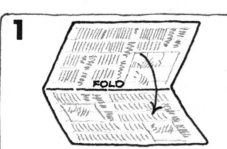

Take a large sheet of newspaper or a double sheet from a small newspaper. Fold it in half.

2

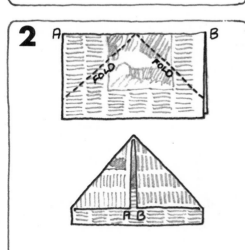

Fold the two top corners so that they meet in the middle.

3

Fold up the remaining edge on both sides. Use sticky tape to hold the paper in position.

4

You can decorate this hat by making a tissue paper tassle. Cut a strip of tissue paper in a fringe all along one edge. Roll up the strip and screw the uncut edge together tightly. Let the cut ends hang free. Stick this tassle into the top of the hat.

The playful cat

Shirley was busy knitting a warm winter scarf for her
favourite doll. The only trouble was, Fluff the kitten,
wanted to play with the wool, too. As the ball of wool
bounced on the floor beside Shirley's stool, Fluff would
jump on it.

'Fluff, stop it,' Shirly told him crossly. But Fluff
wouldn't listen.

In the end, Shirley complained to her mother.

'He's only a kitten, Shirley,' her mother said. 'He wants
to play. I tell you what, I'm sure I've got an old ball of
wool somewhere. Perhaps if I give that to Fluff he'll leave
you alone.'

Shirley put her knitting down and went with her mother
to look for the wool. They soon found a bright pink ball of
wool.

'I think Fluff would like that,' Shirley said.

When they went downstairs again, they were just in time
to rescue Shirley's knitting from Fluff.

'Here, Fluff,' Shirley said, showing him the bright pink
wool. 'This is for you.'

Fluff pounced on the pink wool and in no time at all he
was rolling over and over on the floor, the wool wrapped
around his little paws. Then Shirley was able to finish her
knitting in peace.

The band

It wasn't fair. All the friends were in the new band except for Howard. He wasn't in it because he didn't have a musical instrument. Bill had borrowed his sister's banjo. Charlie had been given a drum for his birthday. Guy had a tambourine. Jim had found a mouth organ. So that just left Howard.

The band called themselves the Famous Four. They weren't famous yet, but Bill said they would be one day. They planned to put on a concert for their parents and friends soon.

Howard so wanted to be part of the band. He told his problem to Mr Williams in the sweetshop, who said that when he was a lad, he wrapped tissue paper round a comb and blew. It made a wonderful sound.

'That's a wonderful idea,' said Howard, and he rushed home to find a comb and some tissue paper. It sounded great! He hurried round to Charlie's garage where the Famous Four were practising.

'Look, I've got a musical instrument,' he shouted. When his friends saw the comb and tissue paper they laughed, but they soon stopped when Howard started to play.

'You're one of us now,' said Bill. 'We'll have to change our name to the Famous Five!'

Howard did feel proud.

Late again

Every morning Mr Robinson took his children to school and every morning Mr Robinson, Brian Robinson, Angela Robinson and Judith Robinson rushed out of the house at the last minute. They were always late!

One morning the Robinsons were even later than usual. It was a very cold morning and none of the children wanted to get out of bed. It was so cold outside the bedclothes.

When they did get up they discovered that their mother had made some lovely hot porridge. But the porridge was *so* hot it took a long time to eat.

When they all finally tumbled out of the house they were already ten minutes later than they should have been. Mr Robinson rushed up to his car. But when he saw it he gave a great big groan. 'Oh no,' he said, 'just look at the car. It will take ages to get the windows clear.' For the windows were all white with frost.

At last Mr Robinson finished scraping off the frost and they all jumped into the car. But it was so cold that the car didn't want to start. It just made a horrible clanking noise. It made such a loud noise that Mr James over the road came out to see what was happening. 'I think we better give you a push,' he said.

So the children jumped out and they and Mr James pushed the car down the road as fast as they could. At last the engine started.

Of course by then the children were so late for school that Mr Robinson had to take them in and apologize to their teacher. The teacher was rather cross!

When the children got home that evening they saw a strange grey shape outside their house. From a distance it looked just like an elephant sitting down. But when the children got nearer they could see it was a great big grey plastic sheet with something underneath.

'It's a winter coat for the car,' explained Mr Robinson, 'and I've bought something else too – a great big alarm clock to wake us all up. We are not going to be late again. I'm too scared of your teacher!'

Idiot's delight

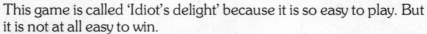

You will need

A pack of cards

This game is called 'Idiot's delight' because it is so easy to play. But it is not at all easy to win.

First, shuffle the cards and then deal four cards in a row, face up. If any of the cards are the same suit, take away the lower one(s), leaving only the highest of that suit. Aces are high in this game – above kings.

Fill in the gap(s) with another card from the pack and if *that* is lower than another in the row of the same suit take that out too.

Continue in this way until you have four cards, none of which you can move. Then deal another four cards on top of the bottom four. Discard wherever possible.

Once you have a pile of two or more cards you can fill in any gaps by moving a card off the top of a pile. This should mean that you can release the card underneath and, with luck, that you might be able to discard it.

Remember – all spaces must be filled from the existing piles if they have two or more cards on, before you deal a new row of cards.

Since aces are high they can never be taken out of the game but they can be moved from the tops of piles into spaces and the object of the game is to end up with just the four aces left in a row.

Patience pairs

You will need

A pack of cards

Shuffle the cards and deal out 12 piles of 4 cards, face down. Put the remaining 4 cards to one side to use later.

Now turn over the top card on all 12 piles and see if there are any pairs: two fives, for example, or two kings. Take away any pairs that you find and then turn up the cards that were underneath them. Look to see if this means you have some more pairs and if so, take *them* away.

Keep on doing this until you have used all the cards from any pile. When this happens, take one from your spare pile so that you can continue.

The object of the game is to sort all the cards into pairs.

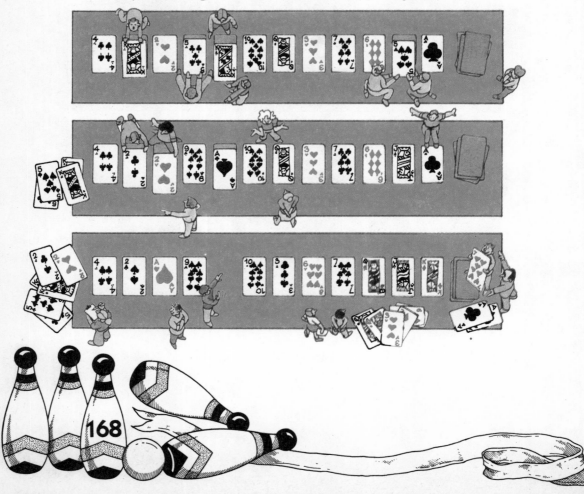

168

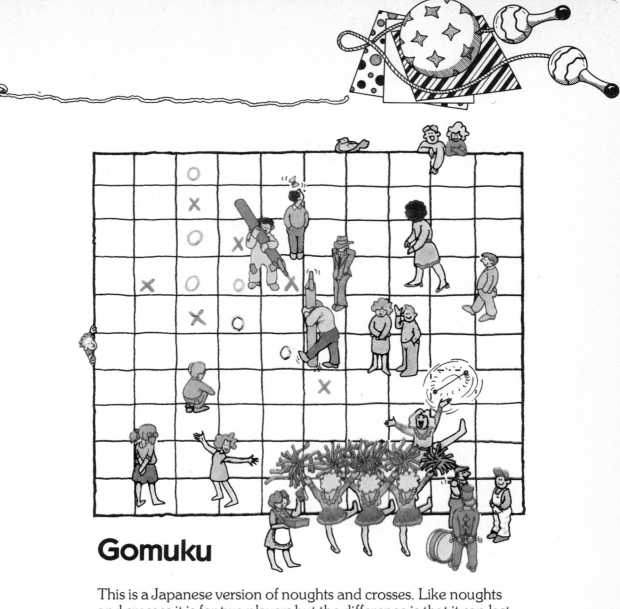

Gomuku

This is a Japanese version of noughts and crosses. Like noughts and crosses it is for two players but the difference is that it can last for hours or minutes, depending on the size of your grid.

To begin with, try playing with a grid of 100 squares – 10 squares across and 10 down. First draw the grid on a piece of paper. Then decide who will draw noughts and who will draw crosses.

Each player takes it in turn to draw a nought or a cross in one of the squares on the grid.

To win the game you must have 5 noughts or crosses in a row, either horizontally, vertically or diagonally. But of course your opponent will try to prevent you from doing this!

New friends

Debbie and her family were moving. 'The removal van is here,' her mummy called up the stairs.

Ebony was snoozing on Debbie's bed. Debbie gently picked up the black cat and popped her in the wicker basket.

At the new house, Debbie put down a saucer of milk, but Ebony rushed upstairs, and crept under Debbie's bed.

Debbie went into the garden and stared at the tall weeds. 'I can't play *here*!' she thought.

A little girl ran into the neat garden next door. 'I'm Tina. Would you like to play with me?' she asked. Eagerly, Debbie ran into Tina's garden.

Later, her mummy called, 'Dinner's ready, Debbie.'

'I must give Ebony her dinner first,' she said, and ran upstairs to fetch her cat. But when Debbie looked under her bed, Ebony wasn't there. Debbie ran downstairs.

'Perhaps she's in the garden. The kitchen door has been open all morning,' said Mummy.

In the garden, Debbie called and called. But Ebony didn't come.

As Debbie sat down to dinner, she saw a white cat come into her garden. 'I wish you were Ebony,' she sighed.

Then she stared. Something moved behind the white cat. It was black.

'It's Ebony! She's made a new friend too!' smiled Debbie happily.

The map-makers

Once there was a village far away in the hills and everybody who lived there worked as a map-maker. The villagers were famed for their skill at drawing maps. People came from far and wide to ask for maps to be drawn.

But suddenly, they could no longer find the way through the hills to the village. And when they found that the maps they had did not show the right way to the village, people decided that there was no point in employing map-makers who did not even know where their own village was.

The villagers were also very confused until they realized that the hills around them had started to move. The way out of the village was never the same from one day to the next. So the people agreed that they would have to do something about it, or they would never again be paid to draw maps and they would starve. They wove huge, thick ropes which they tied round the hills like belts. To these they fastened other ropes which were pegged down with stakes the size of trees. Sure enough, the hills no longer moved.

You may think that this story is nonsense. But even now, in the midst of the great forests that grow up on the hills, you can see the treeless strips where the ropes used to be.

171

The apple farm

Early one morning, Colin was woken by a loud noise underneath his bedroom window. He pulled back the curtain and looked out. There in the street was a red lorry.

Colin rushed downstairs to tell his father. 'The apple lorry is here! It's waiting to take us to the apple farm!'

'Come and eat your breakfast first,' said his mother.

So Colin ate his breakfast, very quickly, and washed and dressed himself and ran outside. Waiting beside the lorry was a little stout man with a round red face. 'Are you Mr Green the apple farmer?' Colin asked him.

'That's right,' said the man. 'Up you get into my lorry now, and off we'll go.'

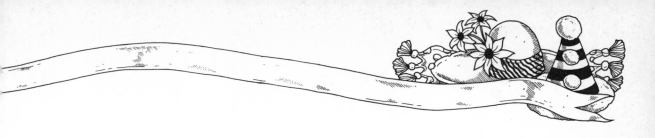

So Colin and his mother and father got in and the red lorry drove out of the town and far into the countryside. At last it stopped at the apple farm. Everywhere there were trees covered with ripe, juicy apples, and children helping their parents to pick the apples and put them into big round baskets.

Mr Green showed them from which tree they were to take the fruit. It had so many apples on it that the branches bowed down to the grass.

Colin's mother and father started to pick the apples and gave them to him to put into a basket. Then, when the bottom branches were empty, Colin's father put a ladder against the tree and helped Colin to climb up to reach the apples on the top branches. Soon the basket was full.

While his father had a rest, Colin played with the other children. They chased each other in and out of the apple trees and played hide and seek in the barn where the farmer kept his red lorry.

At the end of the day Colin was very tired. Mr Green the farmer took them home again in his lorry, and he gave Colin a whole box of ripe juicy apples for himself. But Colin wasn't sure that he wanted them. He had had quite enough of apples for one day!

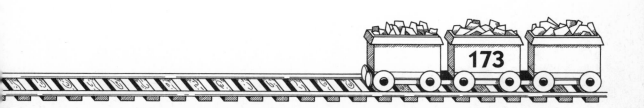

Autumn leaves

'Oh, Mum,' complained Lucy, 'I'm so bored. I've got nothing to do.'

'Why don't you take your puppy for a walk on the heath? It's not raining today and you could ask Kapil, from next door, to go with you,' answered Lucy's mother.

'Do I have to ask him, Mum? He hardly ever says anything.'

'That's because it isn't long since he came here from India,' explained Mum. 'He's not used to speaking English, but you could help him.'

'All right, I'll ask him,' Lucy decided.

'Tell his mother that you won't have to cross the road at all.'

Lucy put on her coat and took Toffee's lead, calling to the puppy as she did. Toffee ran to her, barking excitedly when she saw the lead.

Kapil did not want to go for a walk at first. 'It is so cold in England in autumn. It is so ugly without any leaves on the trees.'

'Do come,' said Lucy, 'it won't be cold taking Toffee for a walk – she tries to run away.'

So Kapil went out with Lucy. 'Race you to the gate to the heath!' she cried, and they both ran off as fast as they could. Kapil got to the gate first.

'Huh, you only won because I had to drag Toffee along,' lied Lucy.

Once they were on the heath, Lucy took off Toffee's lead. Toffee rushed off, barking widly. She disappeared into a huge pile of leaves which had blown against a grassy bank. Lucy ran after her, shouting, 'Come on Kapil!'

Kapil followed, but stood still in surprise when Lucy plunged into the leaves after Toffee. Lucy's smiling face popped up with dusty brown and red leaves stuck in her hair. Kapil laughed and dived in after her.

For the rest of the afternoon they played on the heath. They hid in the leaves and built castles out of them with tunnels in and out. They raced and chased each other and Toffee. There were squirrels and lots of birds to see. Lucy taught Kapil their names.

'They are not the same as the animals in India,' Kapil told Lucy. 'You have to watch out for snakes there.'

At last it was time to go home. 'Come back to my house for tea,' said Lucy.

'Did you like the heath?' Lucy's Mum asked Kapil.

'Oh yes. It was not too hot to run about and there were lots of leaves to play in!' laughed Kapil.

The farmer in the dell

All the children make a circle.

One person is the farmer. He stands in the middle of the circle. All the others join hands and walk round the farmer. This is what they sing:

The farmer's in the dell
The farmer's in the dell
Heigh-ho, heigh-ho
The farmer's in the dell.
The farmer wants a wife
The farmer wants a wife
Heigh-ho, heigh-ho
The farmer wants a wife.

The children stop moving round and the farmer chooses one person to be his wife. She goes into the middle with him, and the others move round them in a circle, singing:

The wife wants a child
The wife wants a child
Heigh-ho, heigh-ho,
The wife wants a child.

The wife chooses a child from the circle. The game continues
with the following verses of the song:

The child wants a nurse
The child wants a nurse
Heigh-ho, heigh-ho,
The child wants a nurse.

The nurse wants a dog
The nurse wants a dog
Heigh-ho, heigh-ho,
The nurse wants a dog.

We all pat the dog
We all pat the dog
Heigh-ho, heigh-ho,
We all pat the dog.

The game ends with everyone patting the dog. The dog
becomes the farmer in the next round of the game.

177

The cowboy hat

Nicky woke up early on his birthday. It was summer, warm and sunny, and on his bed he could see one of his presents – a smart cowboy hat.

Nicky put it on and leaned back happily against the pillows. He fired an imaginary gun into the air.

'Ouch!' said a cross, prickly voice. Nicky found that he was looking at an enormous cactus.

'Here's a horse for you to ride,' said the cactus.

'But I don't know how to ride a horse,' said Nicky.

'Please yourself,' said the cactus, and vanished. Nicky straightened his hat and clambered on to the horse – and he was at a rodeo show! It was hot and dusty with crowds of people there. They cheered him as his horse galloped about, and he brandished his pistol and whirled his lasso.

Suddenly the horse bolted. Nicky hung on tightly, and the sound of cheering followed him.

'Hurrah! He's woken up! Happy birthday!' Nicky's brothers were shouting.

'I've been at a rodeo show. It was very hot,' said Nicky.

'No wonder you're hot,' said his mother. 'You're wearing your hat in bed. Wake up – you're going to have an exciting day.'

'I've had an exciting day already,' said Nicky.

A shell zoo

One morning Dominic was feeling rather bored. His big brother and sister had just gone back to school after the long summer holidays and he was missing them.

'Why don't you play with some of your toys?' asked Mummy.

'It's no fun without Jill and Patrick,' Dominic said.

His mother thought for a while and then she said, 'I know what you can do. Have you still got all the shells we collected on holiday this year?'

'Yes,' said Dominic, 'but what can I do with them?'

'You can make things,' said Mummy. And while Dominic fetched the shells she hunted through the kitchen drawer and found a tube of glue.

'Look for a big round shell,' she said. Dominic found a big round shell.

'Now look for five little shells,' Mummy said. Dominic hunted through the shells and found five little ones.

Mummy stuck the five little shells to the big round one. 'Look,' she said, 'a tortoise.'

'Can I make one?' asked Dominic.

'Of course,' said Mummy. 'And see if you can think of some other animals to make too.'

By the time Jill and Patrick came home, Dominic had a whole shell zoo to show them.

Baby animals

Graham went to stay with his auntie on her farm for his spring holidays. Living in the city, he had never stayed on a farm before. 'What will it be like?' he thought as he arrived there.

When he saw how big the bull was, he was scared, and when he saw how fierce the large cockerel was, he backed away, and when the geese hissed at him he ran and hid under the kitchen table.

'You'll soon get used to all the animals, Graham,' said his auntie laughing.

'No I won't,' insisted Graham. 'They are all either too big or too fierce.'

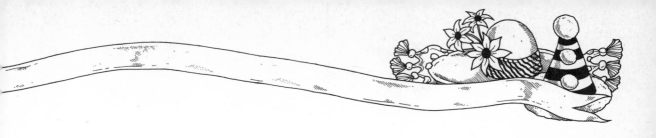

'Then tomorrow morning, if you get up early, you can help me feed all the little animals,' said Auntie. Graham was puzzled – he hadn't seen any 'little' animals.

The following morning, Graham got a surprise. First his auntie took him into a special cowshed. 'Don't forget that it is spring. Spring is when all the animals are having their babies,' she said.

'Oh how sweet,' said Graham as he saw the tiny calf feeding from its mother. 'I think I like cows after all.'

Then they went into a heated place where there were hundreds of tiny fluffy chicks. Graham was allowed to hold one in his hands. It was soft and yellow. 'I think I like chickens after all,' Graham decided.

Next they fed the ducks and geese on the pond. Graham saw some baby goslings and ducklings swimming along with their mothers. 'I like geese as well now,' said Graham as he threw them some small crumbs of bread.

'Auntie, I like being on a farm,' said Graham at the end of his visit. 'May I come again next spring? I'm not so frightened of the big animals any more either.'

'Yes of course you can, and next year you can even help me to feed the bull,' laughed his auntie.

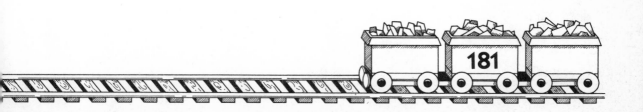

181

One string mobile

1

Draw round a saucer on the card.

2

Cut out the circle and draw a happy face on one side of it.

Of course you don't have to make faces. You can make a single string mobile of a flower, fish or bird.

3

Draw a sad face on the other side.

4

Make a small hole in the top of the circle. Thread some string through and hang your mobile up. The face will change from happy to sad as the mobile turns.

Hanging in a line

You can hang any pieces of card, one beneath the other, and they will turn slowly as long as the pieces of card are joined in the middle. Paint the pieces of card and then join them with thin string.

YOU WILL NEED
Thin card
Thin string
Scissors
Your paint box, felt pens or crayons

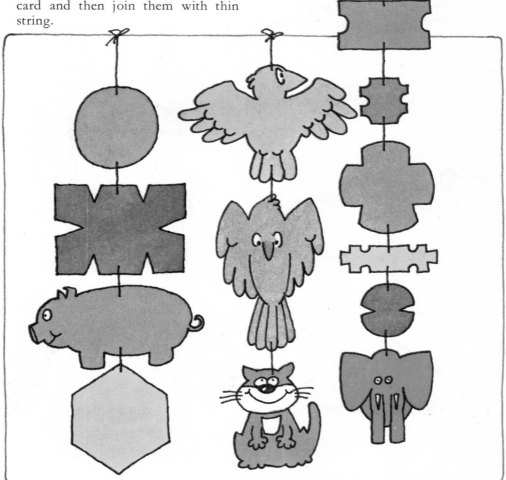

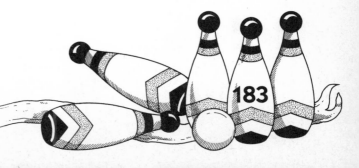

Shiny mobile

YOU WILL NEED
Thin card
Tin foil
Plastic drinking straw
Thin string
Needle and thread
Scissors
Eggcup
Non-toxic glue
Pencil

1

Using an eggcup to draw round, cut out twelve small circles of thin card and twenty-four circles of tin foil. Stick a foil circle on both sides of each piece of card.

2

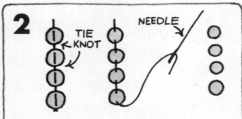

TIE KNOT

NEEDLE

Thread the circles together in fours using a needle.

3

Thread a length of thin string through a plastic drinking straw and tie the ends of the string together.

4

Tie the rows of foil covered circles to the straw. Hang up your mobile and watch the foil circles catch the light as they move.

Badges and brooches

YOU WILL NEED
Thin card
Safety pins
Eggcup
Scissors
Sticky tape
Scraps of felt, odd beads, sequins, shells etc
Non-toxic glue
Your paint box, felt pens or crayons
Pencil

1

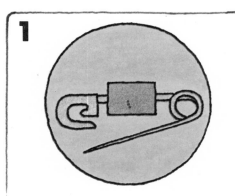

Put an eggcup on a piece of thin card and draw round it. Cut out the circle of card and tape a safety pin to the back of it.

2

Now you can paint or decorate your badge however you like – perhaps with your name or just with a funny face or a pattern.

3

If you have some small pieces of felt you can cover the cardboard base in felt and make felt faces.

4

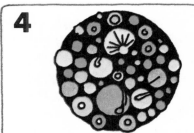

If you want to make a brooch, you can stick beads, sequins or even small shells to the cardboard base.

The swimming pool

It was a hot, sunny afternoon. Ginny's mother and father were sitting at the end of the garden, asleep. All Ginny's friends had gone away to the seaside for their summer holidays. Ginny wished that she was at the seaside. Then she could practise swimming. She paddled in the shallow stream at the bottom of the garden. If only it were deeper!

As she stood still, she noticed how the water got deeper where her legs stopped it flowing downstream. Of course! She could build a dam across the stream to make a pool.

Ginny carefully started to carry large stones from the old wall by the stream. She placed them one by one until there was a row right across the stream. Already, the water was starting to get deeper. Then she brought smaller stones to fill in the gaps between the big rocks. After that, Ginny crossed to the wood on the other side of the stream and collected sticks and twigs. She piled these up behind the rocks and plastered mud over them.

By this time there was only a trickle of water flowing past her dam. Ginny had been careful to build it wider than the stream and high enough, so that a wide, deep pool could form. The pool would soon be deep enough to sit in up to her waist in water, even if she wouldn't be able to swim in it yet. She was rather dirty after all her work, so she decided to go and put on her swimming costume.

A few minutes later, she came back into the garden. As she did so, her mother suddenly jumped up out of her chair, screaming. 'Ralph! Ralph!' she shouted at Ginny's father. 'There's a flood!'

'What! What's happening?' he muttered sleepily.

'Oh dear,' thought Ginny. 'I think I'm in trouble.'

'Ginny!' shouted her father.

186

'Yes Dad?'

'Did you build that dam?'

'Well, yes, I suppose I did,' admitted Ginny.

'Now you can *un*-build it then,' her father told her. 'All the plants and animals below the dam would die without any water. You could also have done lots of damage by flooding the fields and gardens above the dam.'

So Ginny and her father broke down the dam. At least she had the excitement of seeing the water gush through the narrow opening they had made, but then the whole dam was washed away. However, Dad promised to take Ginny to the open-air swimming pool the next day.

Woolly ball

YOU WILL NEED
Thin cardboard
Wool
Darning needle
Scissors
Large glass or mug
Eggcup
Pencil

1

CUT OUT

Draw round a large glass or mug on to a piece of thin cardboard. Cut out the circle of card.

2

CUT OUT

Place an eggcup in the middle of this circle of card. Draw round the eggcup and cut that circle out of the card. You now have a ring of card.

Make a second ring exactly the same as the first.

3

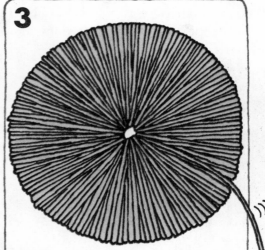

Put the two rings on top of each other and wind wool evenly around them both until the hole in the middle is nearly full. When you can't get any more wool through the hole by hand, continue winding using a darning needle.

DARNING NEEDLE

188

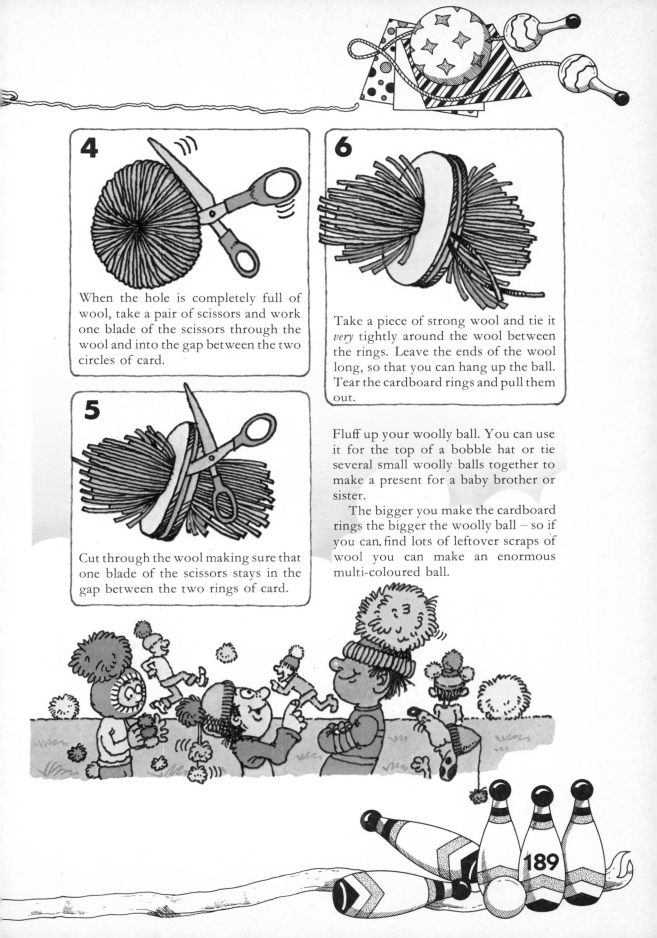

4

When the hole is completely full of wool, take a pair of scissors and work one blade of the scissors through the wool and into the gap between the two circles of card.

5

Cut through the wool making sure that one blade of the scissors stays in the gap between the two rings of card.

6

Take a piece of strong wool and tie it *very* tightly around the wool between the rings. Leave the ends of the wool long, so that you can hang up the ball. Tear the cardboard rings and pull them out.

Fluff up your woolly ball. You can use it for the top of a bobble hat or tie several small woolly balls together to make a present for a baby brother or sister.

The bigger you make the cardboard rings the bigger the woolly ball – so if you can, find lots of leftover scraps of wool you can make an enormous multi-coloured ball.

Rabbits!

'Don't our cabbage seedlings look nice?' said Emily to her brother Nicholas. 'Soon they'll grow into fresh green cabbages. Won't Daddy be pleased!'

When Daddy got home from work at teatime they took him into the garden to show him the two neat rows of little green leaves.

But Daddy looked very puzzled. 'Baby cabbages?' he said. 'I can only see grass and a few weeds.'

Emily said to Nicholas, 'Something ate those baby cabbages and I'll bet it was rabbits!'

So the next morning they both got up extra early to see.

'Just look through this window,' gasped Emily. 'There are lots of baby rabbits nibbling everything – with two big rabbits on guard.'

'We must chase them away,' said Nicholas, and they both dashed outside.

When they told Dad who had eaten the cabbages, he got some green garden netting to spread over the next lot of seedlings.

Tibs the cat helped guard the seedlings too. She sat on the wall and kept a look out for baby rabbits.

190

The butterfly bush

'We're having tea with Aunt Pat today, Tim,' said Mother. 'She has a butterfly bush in her garden.'

Tim was puzzled. Butterflies don't grow on bushes. Butterflies come from caterpillars. Everyone knows that.

During tea Tim kept looking out of the window, but he couldn't see a butterfly bush anywhere.

'Tim can't wait to see your butterfly bush,' said Mother.

So after tea Aunt Pat took him up to the top of the garden. 'There it is,' she said. 'That big bush with the clusters of tiny purple flowers.'

The bush looked like a magic picture – brightly coloured butterflies dancing in and out of the long branches, settling on the flowers, opening and closing their wings in the sunshine.

'I know why it's called a butterfly bush now,' said Tim. 'Butterflies don't grow on it, but they like visiting it.'

When it was time to go home Tim said, 'I wish we had a butterfly bush in our garden.'

'Shall we plant one in our garden?' said Mother.

'Yes please,' said Tim. 'My very own butterfly bush.'

Donkey rescue

Gino was very happy. He was going to visit his cousin Peta all by himself. Gino and Peta lived in Italy, high up in the mountains. Gino lived in a little village on one side of a mountain and Peta lived in a village on the other.

The sun was shining and the snow sparkled on the pathway over the little mountain. Gino was not alone. Walking beside him was his grey donkey, Julietta. She was happy too – she had just had an enormous feed. Gino sung as he walked and Julietta hee-hawed to show that she liked Gino's singing. Neither of them were looking at the pathway. Suddenly Gino screamed. His foot had slipped off the pathway and into a little gulley filled with snow. He wasn't in pain but his foot was stuck fast.

192

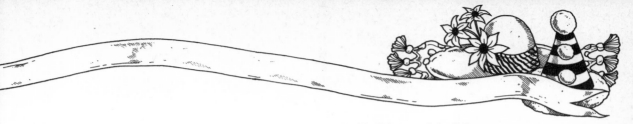

'O Julietta, what am I going to do?' Gino said. 'No one may come this way all day and I'm already getting cold.' Julietta hee-hawed to show she understood and then suddenly trotted off over the mountain path and disappeared.

'Oh don't leave me Julietta,' cried Gino. 'Where are you going?' But she had gone. Gino was very sad and worried and cried a little. He tugged at his foot but it wouldn't move at all.

It seemed to Gino that he had been there a long time when he heard footsteps on the pathway. 'Help, I'm here, help me,' he cried. Suddenly, over the crest of the little mountain, Julietta appeared. Gino couldn't believe his eyes for sitting on her back was his cousin Peta with Uncle Dino following close behind.

'Well young man, you have got yourself in a fix haven't you?' said Uncle Dino. 'But don't worry we'll soon have you out.'

Slowly, he lifted the rock which was trapping Gino's foot. Uncle Dino felt Gino's foot carefully. 'No bones broken,' he said. 'Have a drink of this to warm you up.' In a flask he had some steaming hot, sweet chocolate.

'But how did you know where I was?' said Gino.

'A certain grey donkey came trotting up our path,' said Uncle Dino. 'She made such a racket that we had to follow her.'

'O Julietta, thank you,' said Gino, planting a big kiss on her shaggy mane.

Memory game

You will need:
a tray
pencils
paper
objects from around the house

Most party games are noisy when there are a lot of children. If you feel like something quieter, try the Memory Game. All your guests will be as quiet as mice while they are playing it.

Before the party lay out twelve or more objects on a tray.

You could choose such things as a hairbrush, a button, a candle, an apple, a milk jug and so on.

When you are ready to play the game, carry the tray in to your guests. Tell them to look at it closely for one minute and to memorize all the objects. Take the tray away and hand out some paper and a pencil to each player and ask them all to write down as many objects as they can remember. They can have a few minutes to do this.

They can then swap papers with each other and tick the correct answers as you give them. The winner is the person with the most correct objects.

Hot and cold

Play this guessing game in a room at home. All your party guests can join in.

One player goes out of the room. The other players stay there and decide on an object for him to guess. He is then called back into the room. He has to try and find the object. As he moves about, the other players say 'Cold' when he is far away from the object, 'Warm' and 'Warmer' when he is getting nearer to it and 'Hot' when he is very close.

The guesser has three chances to say what the object is. It is a good idea to wait until he hears that he is hot because he has a better chance of making the right guess.

Everyone has a turn at guessing.

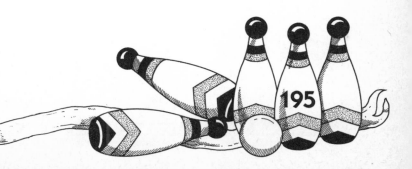

Fort Johnson

The Johnsons were having a new freezer delivered. When some men staggered up the path carrying the heavy package, Jeremy and Robbie were playing cowboys and Indians in the garden. When they saw Mummy putting the huge cardboard box outside the kitchen door, they asked if they could have it.

They tugged and pulled it into their shed, and began to scurry up and down the garden carrying paint pots and scissors. They painted black and brown stripes on the sides of the box and cut a door in the front. They found some old shoe boxes to make into look-out towers and used one of the bean-sticks from the vegetable patch as a flagpole.

Mummy had been far too busy to notice all the activity, and she was very surprised when Robbie rushed in and asked for something to use as a flag for their fort. When she peeped into the shed a little later, she found Robbie and Jeremy sitting inside the fort busily trying to choose a name for it.

'How about Fort Johnson?' asked Mum, as she tied the flag to the pole. So, Fort Johnson it became.

The stone lion

Benjamin, a well behaved lion, was asked to guard the entrance to a palace because one of the stone lions who usually sat outside the doors was having his nose mended.

This was a great honour for Benjamin and he willingly took up his position, sitting on his hind legs and staring out at the world.

He'd been given a list of 'Don'ts' . . .

Don't growl at visitors.

Don't scratch.

Don't lie down.

Don't blink.

In other words, behave at all times like a stone lion.

Benjamin performed his duty day in day out until he really did begin to feel like a stone lion.

One day a van arrived to return the real stone lion, which now had a new nose. Benjamin could hardly move because he'd been sitting still for so long.

It took three weeks before he felt really lively again. And ever afterwards he was known in the jungle for his ability to sit very, very still!

Why don't you try being a stone lion?

Rupert rat

There were six white rats living in a zoo. The keeper knew
them all by their names, which were Rupert, Charlie, Daisy,
Martha, Paula and John. Their cage was large with plenty of
corners to hide in and they were given two good meals a
day. So they were well looked after. But they did sometimes
wish they could run into the wide world and see where the
people who stared in at them lived.

One day the keeper left the door of the cage open by
mistake. Daisy quickly spotted it and ran out, followed by
the others. They found themselves in the passageway that
ran behind their cage. Rupert sat down by a big door near a
little dark hole in the floor. Suddenly the door opened, the
keeper came in and shut it behind him quickly. It was now
or never for escape! Rupert darted down the hole. Just in
time. All the other rats were caught.

Rupert began to get tired and hungry. The tunnel
seemed so large and seemed to go on for ever. Every so
often his tunnel turned and was joined by others. So he was
completely lost. He saw other rats. They were all brown or
black and looked fierce, with eyes that gleamed in the dark.

Rupert tried to catch some pieces of cabbage that were

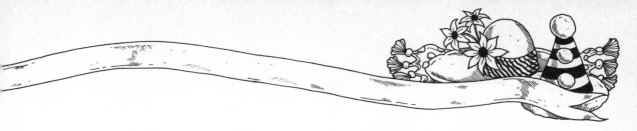

floating past, but a big brown rat got them first and pushed Rupert into the water. It was cold. But the sides were covered with green slime and too slippery to climb out. So Rupert floated down with the current.

Just as he had begun to give up hope the water from the drain swept into a big river and out into the daylight. Rupert saw an old black boot floating along and he climbed on the toe, getting a little warmer and drier in the sunshine.

The boot reached the side of the river. Rupert jumped off and sat in the grass. A lot of people were sitting there and talking, which frightened Rupert a bit, but there were crumbs on the ground so he crept forward and ate some.

Suddenly he was in complete darkness again! Someone had put their hat on top of him. Then a little boy's hand caught Rupert firmly. He was a prisoner again.

But the little boy took Rupert home and he was given a big cage with some hamsters for company and *three* good meals a day. So he did not try to escape again!

Throwing the discus

You will need

Some paper plates
A newspaper
Your crayons or felt pens

Put an open newspaper down on the floor at one end of the room and draw a 'bull's-eye' circle in the middle of it.

Everyone should stand at a point marked on the other side of the room and take turns to try to get their paper-plate 'discus' on to the paper.

Throw the 'discus' by holding it flat and flicking your wrist so that it skims through the air.

Hurling the javelin

You will need

Some drinking straws
A newspaper
Your crayons or felt pens

If you've been playing 'throw the discus' you can use the same target. Stand on one side of the room and hurl your drinking-straw 'javelins' towards the bull's eye!

A Christmas lamb

On the moors, farmers dread heavy snowfalls, because of the danger to their sheep.

One Christmas Eve, very late, Dick's father came into the kitchen from the farmyard. The snow on his coat melted in the warmth, and made puddles on the stone floor.

'I'm still a sheep missing,' he sighed, 'but I'd better have a bite, before I search again.'

Dick finished his soup in silence. His father was tired, he knew. Mother put out more soup, and Dick quietly slipped away. Outside, the wind bit into his face, and the snow stuck in his eyes.

'Come on Scamp,' he said to his dog. 'Let's go and find that poor sheep.'

It was a while before anyone realized Dick was missing. 'The stupid boy!' said his father, upset. 'Doesn't he know he can be buried – just like the sheep?' And he set off to fetch him back.

Dick was weary. The snow made walking difficult. But Scamp was full of enthusiasm, and urged Dick ahead.

Scamp found the sheep behind a boulder and barked excitedly. Dick sank down beside the ewe thankfully. 'Let's have you home, old girl,' he said, imitating his father. But she wouldn't move. Dick tugged and pulled, but the sheep stayed put.

Then Dick heard his father's voice, drifting through the snowflakes. 'Here, Dad!' he yelled.

His father rushed up, stumbling through the snow. 'So you found her?' he said, surprised.

'Scamp did,' said Dick. 'But look, she won't move!'

'I'll soon have her,' said Dad, then he scolded Dick, hard.

'But Dad, I wanted to help you.'

'Aye, but when you're older lad. Not this weather, nor this late hour.'

He took hold of the sheep, and lifted her up in strong arms. They both stared in wonder. For there, was a little tiny lamb.

'Well I never!' Dad exclaimed. 'We'd better get them back, quickly.'

'I'll keep the lamb warm,' said Dick.

'A while longer,' said his father, 'it would have been too late.'

In the distance, the church clock struck twelve, its chimes echoing over the hills.

'Merry Christmas!' said Dick, laughing.

His father turned and smiled at him. 'Merry Christmas, Son.'

Mother was at the door to greet them. 'Thank goodness you're safe!' she cried.

'Merry Christmas!' grinned Dick. And he handed her a present – a tiny, woolly lamb.

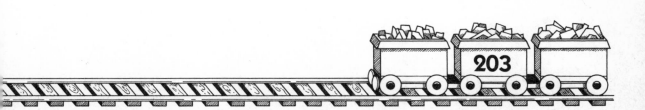

The fishing trip

Hong Kong harbour is crowded with boats, and Kun-fu's home floats in the harbour too. He lives on a Chinese fishing-junk; a large wooden boat with batwing sails.

'Come!' said his father one evening, 'a school of fish has been sighted! We must prepare for a night of fishing.'

When all was ready, the large sails, which almost blocked out the red sunset, were unfurled. One by one, the junks pulled out; and sailed through the harbour entrance, into the rolling waves of the South China Sea.

When dark, the Chinese fishermen hung bright lanterns on the bows of their junks, to attract fish. Kun-Fu thought they looked like sparkling jewels. They slowly trawled through the night, then, 'Heave in!' shouted his father, and Kun-Fu helped to drag the nets aboard.

They were heavier than usual. Then Kun-Fu saw why. 'Shark!' he cried. 'We have a shark!'

In the nets was a large shark, which fought and turned as it came to the surface. 'Get it!' shouted his father.

But with a leap, the shark splashed back into the sea. Still, it had driven hundreds of fish into their nets.

They had the largest catch, ever.

Cathy's plant

Cathy loved Grandad's greenhouse. It was another world in there, all warm and moist. There were plants in pots, plants in boxes, tiny plants and large plants.

One day Grandad said to her, 'Would you like to take a small plant home, and grow it yourself?'

'Oh thank you!' said Cathy. 'Will it have beautiful flowers like yours?'

'Yes,' said Grandad. 'Bring it to show me, when it does!'

At home, Cathy put her plant on a window-sill. There, she looked after it and watered it.

A few days later, she noticed *two* little plants in her pot. And one was growing faster than the other. She remembered what Grandad had told her – never have two plants in one pot. So she pulled the smaller one out.

The little plant that was left grew well under Cathy's care, and became quite large.

She waited hopefully for a flower-bud, but none came.

Then Mummy said, 'I'm sure that plant is not the same as the ones Grandad is growing.' Cathy felt quite worried.

'Bring it to show me,' said Grandad, when they told him. So they wrapped it carefully, and took it to his greenhouse.

When Grandad saw it, he laughed loudly. 'Oh Cathy!' he laughed, 'has it stung you?'

'Stung me?' echoed Cathy, and Mummy stared.

'Yes,' said Grandad. 'What you've grown here is – a nettle!'

'Oh dear!' said Cathy. 'I must have pulled out the wrong seedling!'

Messy pictures

It is fun to make a mess sometimes – just make sure you clear up afterwards! The best thing about messy pictures is that no one can ever be sure how they are going to turn out.

YOU WILL NEED
Sheets of plain paper
Drinking straw
Thin card
Flour
Water
Your paint box
Old comb or fork
Mixing bowl
Scissors
Spoon

Put a lot of runny paint on a piece of paper. Blow at it through a straw so the paint moves about. That way you can make an interesting 'blow painting'.

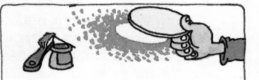

Make a spatter painting by this method: hold a brush full of drippy paint over a sheet of paper. Tap the brush hard and watch the paint spatter! If you like you can cut out some card shapes, place them on top of your paper, spatter the paint over them and then pick the shapes up to leave a pattern.

To make a fold painting, make a crease down the middle of a piece of paper by folding it in half. Put large, wet splodges of paint on one side of the paper. Fold the paper in half and press the two sides together firmly. Open the paper and see what kind of pattern you've made.

206

If you want to make a paste picture you have to make a flour and water paste first. Just slowly add water to a small amount of flour in a bowl, stirring all the time until you have a thick paste. Colour the paste with paint then spread the mixture all over a thick piece of paper. Now make patterns in the paste — with your fingers, with an old comb, with a fork — or with anything else you can think of. You could use an old glass or even your whole hand.

Murals

A mural is a painting as big as a wall! It's not easy to find that much paper but ask around for old pieces of wallpaper or sheets of thick wrapping paper. It's best to make a mural in the summer when you can work outside. Ask if you may tack the paper to a wooden fence with drawing pins — then you can paint on a really large scale.

One of the things you could put on
your mural is a life-size self-portrait.
Get a friend to draw round you then
you can colour yourself in!

Dressing up

Mum had been an actress once. Eric said he would like to be an actor one day. Mum saved all her bits of old make-up for him to play with.

The part he liked to play best was that of a ghost. He used some of Mum's face pack. This was white and set quite hard on his face. He had to be careful not to get it round his eyes and mouth. He dressed up in an old white sheet and Mum said he looked quite frightening. Especially when he walked with stiff arms and legs.

Eric and his sister, Jenny, were allowed to use all the old clothes from the attic for dressing up. Jenny wore a big floppy hat and a long dress with lots of frills. She wore a pair of her mum's high heeled shoes which she stuffed with newspaper so that they wouldn't fall off.

Eric dressed up as a clown too. He borrowed Dad's old suit, which was much to big for him, and a bowler hat from Grandad. This was too big as well, so it fell over his nose so that he couldn't see. He put lipstick on his nose and on his cheeks and made everyone laugh with his funny walk.

210

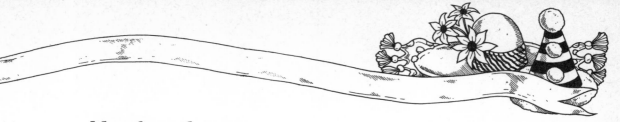

Under the sea

Under the sea no one liked Garry Crab. 'You're crabby!' said the starfish. 'You're always cross and grumpy.'

Poor Garry Crab!

'Cheer up!' said Jerry Jellyfish. 'You're not the only one who isn't liked. No one likes me either.'

The starfish had to agree. 'You're often bad-tempered,' the starfish told Jerry Jellyfish. 'And when you are in one of your bad tempers – you sting. No one likes being stung.'

Garry Crab looked thoughtful. 'I don't mind being stung,' he said. 'You see, I don't feel stings. My hard shell protects me. Perhaps you and I should be friends, Jerry. We'll live together in that empty cave.'

Jerry Jellyfish looked a little less cross than usual, and the two new friends went to the cave straightaway to set up home together.

Garry Crab was pleased to have a new friend who liked him. In fact, he was so pleased that he wasn't crabby or cross or grumpy any more.

Jerry Jellyfish was so pleased to have a new friend that he forgot all about being bad-tempered. Because he wasn't bad-tempered, he didn't sting any more.

Soon all the underwater folk liked Garry and Jerry – even the starfish!

The sticky buds

Billy was sending a birthday card to his gran. Her birthday was in the spring and he had chosen a lovely card covered in flowers.

'I will write Gran's address on some paper. Then you can copy it on to the envelope,' said Billy's mum.

Billy was excited. It was the first time he had written an address on an envelope.

'Very good, dear,' smiled Mum when he'd finished. 'Now you will need to seal it up. Lick the flap on the back of the envelope and stick it down.'

So Billy licked the envelope flap very, very well, and then he pressed it down.

But it came undone!

'You've licked it so well you've licked all the sticky-stuff off,' said Mum laughing.

Just then Billy's sister Beverley came in holding some twigs with big brownish green buds on. The buds looked as if they'd been dipped in a treacle pot!

'They're sticky buds,' said Beverley. 'When they open up, they will grow into beautiful little horse chestnut leaves.'

Beverley put the buds down on the table and she and Mum went to find a vase to put them in.

'I wonder if they'll stick this envelope flap,' said Billy touching the sticky buds. 'They feel very sticky.' And Billy rubbed one of the buds against the envelope.

But no, still the flap came undone and the bud left a nasty, sticky, brown mark on the envelope!

When Mum came back and saw what Billy had done, she said, 'That was a good idea Billy, but I'm afraid sticky buds can't really be used instead of glue! You'll have to write another envelope for Gran's card.'

Three little kittens

Three little kittens,
They lost their mittens,
And they began to cry,
'O Mother dear,
We sadly fear,
That we have lost our mittens.'

'What! Lost your mittens,
You naughty kittens!
Then you shall have no pie.
Mee-ow, mee-ow,
Then you shall have no pie.'

214

The three little kittens,
They found their mittens,
And they began to cry,
'O Mother dear,
Come here, come here,
For we have found our mittens!'

'What! Found your mittens,
You good little kittens,
Then you shall have some pie.
Purr, purr, purr, purr,
Then you shall have some pie.'

The three little kittens
Put on their mittens,
And soon ate up their pie.
'O Mother dear, we greatly fear
That we have soiled our mittens.'

'What! Soiled your mittens,
You naughty kittens.'
And they began to cry,
'Mee-ow, mee-ow,'
And they began to cry.

The three little kittens,
They washed their mittens,
And hung them out to dry.
'O Mother dear, come here, come here,
For we have washed our mittens.'

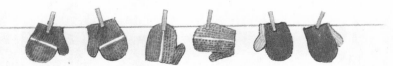

'What! Washed your mittens?
You good little kittens.
Now hush, hush,
I smell a mouse close by,
I smell a mouse close by!'

Strongman

You will need

A large sheet of paper

This is one of those tricks that makes people seethe with fury when they realise how simple it is!

Take a large piece of paper, give it to a friend and ask him to fold it in half eight times.

The chances are that he'll fold it in half, then in half again, then in half again – still quite easily – but by the time he gets to the sixth fold he'll be having difficulties. Then he'll give up!

Now you take the paper, smooth it out again, and show him how it's done.

To fold the paper in half eight times, all you do is fold it in half, open it out again, fold it in half again, open it out again, and so on, eight times!

217

Maggie's budgerigar

'You are the nicest budgerigar in all the world,' said Maggie to her pet budgie Bobby as she played a game with him.

Bobby was perched on top of the table and he was playing ping-pong. Maggie rolled a ping-pong ball towards him, and Bobby pushed it back to her with his beak.

Just then, Maggie's mummy came in. 'How would you like to go on holiday to Australia?' Mummy asked Maggie.

'Oh yes please Mum,' said Maggie. 'Will we go in an aeroplane?'

'Yes,' said Mum, 'and we'll be able to visit Aunty Gwen and Uncle Mike and all your cousins. It will be really exciting.'

Then Maggie said, 'Will Bobby be able to come as well?'

'I'm afraid Bobby can't possibly come with us,' said Mum. Then she had an idea: 'I know – we can ask Gran to look after him until we get back again. How's that?'

Maggie nodded, but secretly she was very sad at having to leave Bobby at home with Gran. And all the way to Australia on the aeroplane she kept thinking about him. 'I hope I don't forget what he looks like,' she said to Mum. 'And I hope Gran will play ping-pong with him and let him fly about.'

Even when they got off the aeroplane and saw the lovely sandy beaches and sparkling sea Maggie still felt a bit sad. But when they got to the farm where her Aunty Gwen and Uncle Mike lived she got a very big surprise. For in all the trees around the farm there seemed to be lots and lots of green birds that looked just the same as Bobby.

'They *are* budgerigars,' said Aunty Gwen. 'Budgerigars live in the trees in Australia, just like sparrows do where you live.'

Then Maggie told them all about her budgerigar called Bobby who could play ping-pong. And she wasn't lonely any longer because it was springtime and there were so many budgerigars to see.

When they got home from their Australian holiday Maggie told Bobby why she hadn't been lonely. 'But those budgerigars weren't as clever as you,' she said. 'They couldn't play ping-pong!'

The little lamb

One cold morning at the end of the winter a little lamb was born. It greeted the world with a cry, 'Baaaaaaa'.

It was a very small lamb and very weak. It found it difficult to stand up on its thin little legs so it just lay in the snow at the edge of the field.

Luckily, soon afterwards, Mr Walker the sheep farmer came along with his dog Gyp. Gyp was a very clever dog and he found the little lamb at once.

'Poor little chap,' said Mr Walker picking up the lamb. 'We'd better take you home.'

When they arrived back at the farmhouse, Judith and Ann, Mr Walker's two little girls, were just finishing breakfast.

'Ohhhh!' they said when they saw the little lamb. They nursed it by the fire while their mother warmed some milk. She put the milk in an old feeding bottle that had been Ann's when she was a baby. Then Judith and Ann took it in turns to feed the lamb.

'We'll keep it here until it gets stronger,' their father said.

The girls *were* pleased with their new pet.

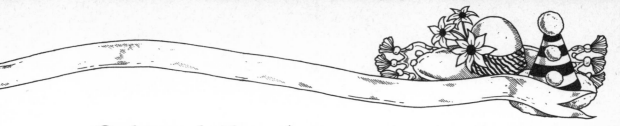

Galumph the giant

Galumph the giant was far too large and clumsy to play with the other children. It always ended in disaster. Twice he'd played football with them. Once he'd kicked the ball, and it had soared right over the whole town. The next time, he'd squashed the ball flat under his boot. Climbing the oak tree – the children's favourite game – was a real joke. The top branch only came up to his knee! So he just sat on his own and watched them play.

One night, there was a tremendous storm. It beat at the windows and blew slates off the roofs and, worst of all, blew the oak tree down. What could the children climb on now?

Galumph had a brainwave. 'Why don't you pretend *I'm* the oak tree,' he bellowed.

The children were delighted. The laces in his boots made fabulous ladders and it was great fun hiding in his pockets and swinging from his tie.

'You're better than the oak tree any day,' said one girl. Galumph didn't dare open his mouth to say thank you because she was sliding down his nose. It would never do if she fell into his mouth! So he just stood very still, children climbing all over him. He was very, very happy.

Going on a trip

This is a game that you can play anywhere. You could be at home, in the car, on a bus, in a train or in the playground at school. You need two players and you can have more if you like.

The first player says 'I'm going on a trip and I'm going to take . . . ' and names an object. The second player has to repeat this and then add another object. The game continues like this, with each person running through the list of objects and adding a new one. As soon as a player misses out an object or mixes up the order he is out of the game. The winner is the last person to be out. She starts the next game.

Quadruped

Here is another game for a long journey in the car. It is easy to play but you must concentrate for a long time.

The idea of the game is to see who can count the most quadrupeds (four-legged animals) during the journey. The person on the right side of the car counts quadrupeds to the right of the road. The person on the left of the car counts quadrupeds on the left-hand side.

You get one point for each animal. It is bad luck if you pass a school – the player on the school side loses all his points. Before you start the game, you can agree on one animal that is worth ten points. It can be any animal you like, but it should be one that is not likely to be seen often, such as a black pig.

Georgina

Sally had been given a cat for her birthday. Mother had told her it was a male cat so Sally called it George.

George soon grew into a very big fat cat who was quite content to sit on the windowsill and watch the world go by.

'There's something wrong with that cat,' Mother said.

'No there isn't, Mummy,' Sally told her. 'He just likes to sit and think.'

A few days later when Sally got home from nursery school she found that George was not in his usual 'thinking' position on the windowsill. She and her mother searched the whole house but there was no sign of dearest George.

By the time Sally's father arrived home they were both upset. There was still no sign of George.

'Tea!' Sally's father suggested to cheer them up. 'I'll go and put the kettle on.' They heard him say, 'This stupid washing machine's stopped working. The door's open.' Then he yelled, 'Come quickly.'

Sally and Mummy ran into the kitchen and there, sitting inside the drum of the washing machine, was George with three tiny kittens!

'George is a father!' shouted Sally. Then again, 'I mean George is a mother! George was a Georgina all the time!'

The Dead Sea

'I've got a surprise for you,' said Ruth's father. 'Today we are going to visit a sea where no one can sink!'

Ruth climbed into the van, and they drove from their home-town of Beersheba all the way to a wide valley of bare rocks. They came down to a big stretch of milky-grey water.

'This is the Dead Sea,' said Ruth's father. 'Now, see if you can sink in that water.'

Ruth waded in. The water felt sticky, and it stung if it splashed on to her mouth or eyes. It tasted very, very salty.

Ruth lay on her back, floating. Her father was right – she couldn't sink. Even if she sat up, as though she was in a chair, she just bobbed about, like a cork.

'You can't sink because of all the salt in the water,' said Ruth's father. 'But because of the salt, nothing can live in the water – that's why it is called the Dead Sea.'

When Ruth got out of the water she found her skin was covered in dry salt, and felt all itchy.

'Now you must have a shower,' said her father. 'After swimming in this sea, you need to wash all over again!'

Sugar the donkey

Barry had always lived in the country. Fields were all around his cottage.

In one of the fields, lived Barry's special friend. A brown donkey.

Barry didn't know his real name, so he called him Sugar, because he loved it so much.

One morning, Barry put two sugar lumps in his trouser pocket and set off to see the brown donkey.

But in the lane, there was no 'Hee-haw' of welcome, and no soft nose poked itself into the little boy's pocket in search of the sugar he knew would be there.

In dismay, Barry stared around.

He looked behind every tree in the field. Then, he looked in the next field, and the next. But there was no sign of the brown donkey.

226

Every morning, Barry put two sugar lumps in his trouser pocket and ran down the lane, hoping that Sugar had come home. But the field was always empty. Barry grew sadder and sadder.

At the end of the week, his Mummy said, 'We are going on holiday today. That will make you feel better.'

Barry had never been to the seaside before. He liked it so much, that he forgot to be sad.

One morning, as he was making a sandcastle, he heard a noise he knew quite well.

'Hee-haw! Hee-haw!'

Barry stared in amazement. A man was walking down the beach leading some donkeys. One of them was *brown*.

'It's Sugar!' cried the little boy. He dropped his spade and eagerly ran towards him.

Sugar had come to be a seaside donkey for the Summer, and his owner told Barry that in the Winter he would be back in his field.

Swimming race

You will need

A bowl of water
Some corks
Some drinking straws

Each player tries to blow a cork across the bowl of water using a straw. You can all blow at once and see whose cork gets across first, or you can time each person and compare notes afterwards.

Water race

You will need

*Glasses of water
Teaspoons*

Players divide into pairs and each pair has a glass of water and a teaspoon. One of the pair 'feeds' water to her partner with the teaspoon, being careful not to spill any. The winners are the first to empty their glass.

Bernie badger

Mother Badger called her family together. 'Winter is nearly here,' she said. 'It is time for our big sleep.'

'What sleep?' asked Bernie, the eldest. His mother told him how they slept until spring, and it was called 'hibernation'.

Bernie was horrified. 'Sleep all that time?' he gasped. 'But I might miss something!' And he firmly refused to hibernate at all. He went to find the hedgehogs to ask them to play. But they were curled in tight, prickly balls – and snoring. The squirrels were fast asleep, too.

'*I'm* not tired,' said Bernie. But as the days passed he yawned and felt lonely.

Then, the first snowflakes began to fall. 'What's this?' he wondered. He gazed up at the swirling flakes, and they stuck on his nose. Before he knew it, he was as white as the world around him.

He didn't like it, and rushed home. 'Just until this white stuff goes,' he told himself, as he crept inside.

Mother Badger shook him. 'Wake up!' she said.

Bernie blinked, then remembered. 'I'm white!' he cried. 'Everything is white!'

They all laughed at him. 'You're dreaming!'

He peeped outside . . . and saw it was springtime.

He had hibernated after all!

Ducks on ice

David was bored. He lived in a little village in the country
and today his friend Andrew was to have visited him, but
Andrew lived in an even smaller village and his mother had
just rung up to say they were snowed in, so Andrew couldn't
come.

'Why don't you go down to the pond and feed the ducks?'
said David's mother. 'They'll need food in this weather.
Take Skippy, he could do with a walk, but be careful of the
ice on the pond.'

So David, and Skippy his dog, with a *huge* bag of bread
walked down to the village pond. It looked quite magical.
The water was frozen and the overhanging trees sparkled
with icicles.

David spotted the ducks huddled together and Skippy
saw them too. He went bounding over the ice. Suddenly his
legs went 'splat' and he slithered forward on his tummy.

David couldn't help laughing. Poor Skippy looked so
surprised and so funny. He felt much more cheerful and the
poor cold ducks seemed happier too, eating big chunks of
bread and fluffing up their feathers to keep themselves warm.

The hidden track

Walking up to the old mine the summer visitors waved to
Megan sitting on her garden wall. They came from the
valley on a narrow gauge railway train, but halfway up the
steep Welsh mountainside the track stopped. Everyone had
to walk the rest of the way.

'I wish the trains went all the way to the mine,' Megan
said to Mr Jones, the train driver. 'They would steam right
past our house.'

'When I was a boy the track did go to the mine,' said Mr
Jones.

When Megan heard this she decided to look for the old
railway track. She explored everywhere and was just thinking
it was teatime, when she tripped over something. Hidden in
the long grass lay a length of rusty iron track. She followed
it all the way to the old mine workings.

'Perhaps the line could be opened again,' she said to Mr
Jones, showing him the track the next day.

And it was. For the rest of the year people were hard at
work mending the track and making it safe.

So the following summer Megan was able to wave to the
visitors on the train as it steamed past her garden wall.

232

The magical tea-plant

Long ago on the island of Sri Lanka lived an Emperor who loved tea. His servants knew many secret recipes and visiting princes marvelled at the wonderful tea they were offered.

One day the Emperor pushed aside his seventeenth cup of tea. 'Bring me something new!' he ordered.

But no one could find a new tea to please him. Finally the Emperor offered a sack of gold to the person who found him a delicious new tea.

Far from the palace lived Sula and her grandmother. In their garden grew the most fragrant tea-plant in the world, but they would not sell it, even for a sack of gold.

Two thieves heard of their tea-plant and plotted to steal it. Early one morning they secretly dug up the tea-plant and fled back to the city leaving behind nothing but a single leaf.

Sula and her grandmother wept, and where their tears fell on the leaf, a new tea-plant sprang up.

The thieves did not win the sack of gold, for the stolen tea-plant withered and died in the strange soil.

But each year Sula and her grandmother sent enough tea from their magical tea-plant for the Emperor to have two cups of fragrant tea on his birthday.

233

Beggar my neighbour

You will need:
a pack of cards

You can play this card game with any number up to six. Deal the cards as far as they will go.

The players do not look at the cards. They place them face downwards in a pile on the table in front of them.

The player on the left of the dealer turns the top card of his pile face upwards and puts it in the centre. All the other players do the same. When someone turns up an Ace, King, Queen or Jack, the next player has to pay him with some of her cards. She pays four for an Ace, three for a King, two for a Queen and one for a Jack.

If one of the cards that she pays with is an Ace, King, Queen or Jack, the player on her left must pay her.

When a pay-off is completed, the last person to be paid takes all the cards from the centre and puts them at the bottom of his pile. The winner is the player who collects all the cards in the pack.

Old maid

You will need:
a pack of cards

Nobody likes to be the Old Maid in this game, but it is still a very popular one. Any number can play.

Take one of the Queens out of the pack and deal out the rest of the cards as far as they will go.

Players look at their cards and take out any pairs of cards of the same rank (number). If a player has three cards of the same rank, he throws out two and keeps one.

The dealer offers her cards face down to the player on her left. This player draws a card out. If the card makes a pair with one of his, he puts them both aside with the other pairs. If not, he puts it in with the cards in his hand. Then he offers his hand to the player on his left who draws out a card. Play goes on clockwise around the table until one player is left holding one Queen. This is the Old Maid.

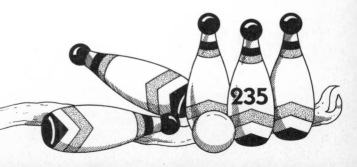

The baby seal

'Come back!' called Mummy Seal, but the baby seal didn't hear. The baby seal didn't *want* to hear. He was having far too much fun! He was chasing such a splendid fish.

On he swam, rushing through the deep sea. Then suddenly the sea narrowed into a river, and Baby Seal became excited. 'I shall catch the fish here,' he thought. 'I'm sure to catch it where the river ends!' And he tried harder, the tide carrying him in as he swam. Soon, the river narrowed to a creek, with boats tied up at either side.

He began to feel a little nervous, swimming underneath the keels of the boats. Then, BAM! He was up against a huge, wooden door. It was the lock gates and he could swim no further. Where was his fish?

It wasn't anywhere to be seen. And with a horrible, sick feeling, the baby seal realised he was lost, miles away from home. He swam around the boats unhappily.

'Oh why,' he thought sadly, 'didn't I listen to Mummy? I should have stopped when she called,' and he sobbed to himself under the water.

Then he remembered Mummy telling him about men, and a shiver ran down his back. 'Beware always of men,' she had said, 'for some men are seal catchers, and will kill you for your fur.'

Baby Seal shuddered. Were there seal catchers here? He raised his head above the water to see. And the boat at the side of him rocked, as a man stepped into it.

236

Before he knew what was happening, the man had reached over the side and caught him. He struggled frantically, but with a lift of strong arms, he was dragged into the boat. He was caught! He was caught!

Fisherman Bob stroked him gently as he spoke. 'Now, now, little chap, don't be frightened, I won't hurt you. It's lucky that I found you for I'm just going fishing, and can take you back to the sea.'

And that's just what he did. Fisherman Bob gave the baby seal a lift in his boat back to the sea, and there he found Mummy Seal again. He doesn't ever disobey her, now.

Pumpkin face

It was the end of October. The days were growing shorter, and already the lawn outside Alison's window was covered with leaves.

'It will soon be Hallowe'en,' said her mother.

'What's Hallowe'en?' asked Alison.

'It's a special night,' her mother told her. 'Long ago, people believed that on Hallowe'en witches came riding through the darkness to peer in through lighted windows.'

'And what did the people do?' asked Alison.

'They carved funny heads out of pumpkins and put them in the windows with candles inside.'

'That must've frightened the bad witches away,' laughed Alison. 'Can we have a pumpkin face in *our* window on Hallowe'en?'

'If you want,' said her mother.

So they bought a round, orange pumpkin from the greengrocer, and Alison's mother scooped out the inside to make it hollow. Then she showed Alison how to cut out two long, slanting eyes, and a round nose, and a wide grinning mouth. Then, on Hallowe'en night, they lit a candle and stood it inside the hollow pumpkin head on the windowsill.

'If *I* were a witch out tonight,' Alison told her mother, 'I'd be so frightened that I'd fly right up into the sky and never come back again!'

The corn dolly

Hannah watched Grandfather thatching his strawstack to keep out the winter rain.

Grandmother came into the stackyard. 'Harvest is nearly over, Hannah, but there's one more job to do.'

Grandmother took Hannah to the cornfield. The prickly stubble crunched beneath their feet. Here and there odd stalks of corn were left standing. Hannah and Grandmother collected them into a bundle.

Back at the farmhouse Grandmother put the cornstalks in water to soften, while she made tea.

'When I was your age, Hannah,' she said, 'the last stalks of corn were made into a corn dolly, and kept in the farmhouse for luck.'

After tea Grandmother started weaving the cornstalks together. She made a long plait which she bent into a horseshoe shape. Then she made a thinner plait with which to hang it on the wall.

'That's not a dolly,' said Hannah, as Grandmother tied a bright red bow to the horseshoe.

Grandmother laughed, 'I always make horseshoes, but you could make a little corn man or even a star.'

She showed Hannah how to make a little corn dolly with the leftover stalks. It was a bit bumpy and lopsided, but Hannah was very pleased with it.

'I'll ask Grandfather to hang it on the stack for luck,' she said.

239

Aeroplane

YOU WILL NEED
6 large cardboard boxes
Large piece of thin card
Scissors
Non-toxic glue or sticky tape
Emulsion paint and large brush
Your paint box, felt pens or crayons

1

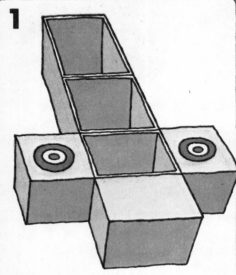

Glue or tape the boxes together like this. You don't have to paint your aeroplane all over but if you do it's best to use emulsion paint. You can use your own paints or crayons to paint on your own airline insignia.

2

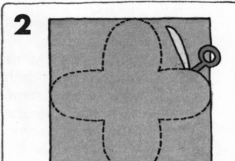

Cut out a propeller from a piece of cardboard and stick it on the front. Paint controls inside the box where you sit.

240

Train

1

YOU WILL NEED
At least four large cardboard boxes
String
Small pieces of thin card
Non-toxic glue or sticky tape
Green emulsion paint and large
  brush
Your paint box, felt pens or crayons
Scissors

Glue or tape two boxes together like this to make the engine. Paint them all over with green emulsion paint. Make wheels and a window from scraps of thin card, paint them in bright colours using your own paints, felt pens or crayons and stick them to the engine.

2

Now the other boxes can be carriages – one for each of your friends. And everyone can decorate his or her own carriage. Make a small hole in the ends of each carriage. Thread string through a hole in two boxes and tie knots on the insides. Join all your carriages together like this.

Flip the kipper

You will need

A sheet of paper for each player
A rolled up newspaper for each player
Your crayons or felt pens
Scissors
String
2 heavy books

This is a game that everyone enjoys. It takes a small amount of time to prepare but it's worth it!

First, draw a large, simple, fish shape on a piece of paper and cut it out. Make as many of these 'kippers' as there are players. You can colour and decorate them if you are making them for a special occasion like a party. Otherwise just give them an eye.

Now line up all the kippers at one end of the room and make a 'finishing line' at the other end with a piece of string on the ground. Hold it in place with two books.

Everyone is given a rolled up newspaper or magazine and at the word, 'Go', they must thwack it down behind their kipper to make the kipper race along. The first person to get their kipper past the finishing line is the winner.

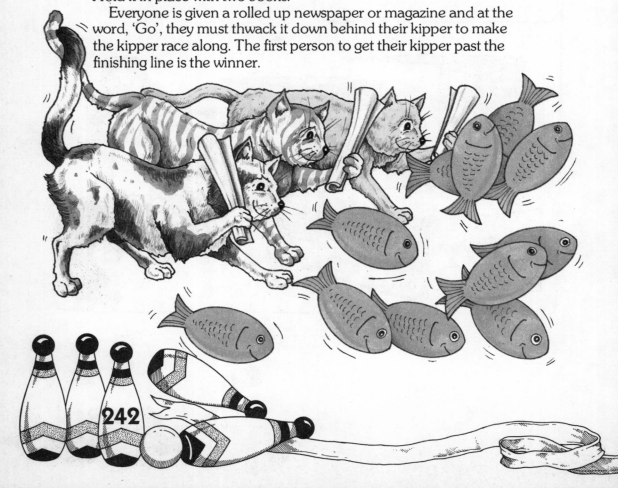

242

Sardines

This game is an old favourite and is always fun to play. It's a bit like a back to front version of hide-and-seek and is best played in a house where there's plenty of room and lots of places to hide.

One person goes off to hide while everyone else stays in one place with their eyes closed and counts to one hundred.

The person who hides should choose a place that's not too small because after the count of one hundred everyone starts to look for her and whenever a player finds her they quietly join her in the hiding place.

At the end of the game everyone is squashed into the hiding place like sardines in a tin, except the last person who is still hunting.

Once the last person finds everyone else the game starts again with the first person to have found the hiding place being the next one to go off and hide.

243

Tommy Tadpole

Tommy Tadpole was discontented. Ever since he had swum to the top of the pond, and had seen the bright colours of the world above the water, he had hated his black coat. How he longed for a coat of brilliant yellow like the kingcups, freckled with green, the colour of the water-lily leaves.

Everyone in the pond was tired of Tommy's grumbles, and they pretended to be busy whenever he swam by. His crowds of brothers and sisters darted off into the weed when he started to talk about green and yellow coats. The water snails stayed in their shells, the water beetles crawled away, and the minnows just laughed, shooting past in a silvery shoal. His only friend was a caddis larva, an ugly little fellow in a mosaic vest made of tiny stones.

'It must be dull living at the bottom of the pond,' said Tommy. 'I'd be bored if I were you.'

'Well, you're not me!' said the caddis larva. 'Anyway, one day I shall grow wings and fly away.'

'I don't believe it,' said Tommy, and he laughed even louder than the minnows.

244

One day he saw the caddis larva climbing slowly up a plant stem.

'It won't be long now,' said the larva cheerfully.

'What won't be long now?' asked Tommy.

'The day when I get my wings and fly away,' he answered. Tommy laughed and turned three quick somersaults.

Next day the caddis larva had climbed half out of the water. Tommy pushed his head out of the water to see what was happening. He was just in time, for the larva had wriggled out of its vest, and now it sat drying a pair of beautiful gossamer wings.

'Is it really you?' asked Tommy in amazement.

'Your turn next,' called the caddis fly as he flew away. Tommy leapt after him, but frogs can't fly and he landed on another lily leaf. He looked at his reflection. It was magnificent!

'I suppose I was so busy grumbling that I never noticed my legs growing and my tail disappearing!' he said to himself.

'I'm a frog!' he told the world in a jubilant croak. 'And your coat is a beautiful green and yellow,' sang the willows.

The scissor man

Not all that long ago, children who sucked their thumbs were told that the scissor man would come along and cut off their thumbs. But this wasn't true at all because the scissor man was really very kind and had never cut off a thumb in his life.

Now the evil emperor, who employed the scissor man, was getting suspicious. 'Next week, you will bring me all the thumbs you've cut off to prove you're doing your job properly,' he said to the scissor man.

Poor Scissor Man! What could he do? It was so cruel to cut off children's thumbs. Then he spied, in a joke-shop window, some false thumbs made out of plastic. 'I wonder . . .' thought the scissor man. Then he went into the shop and bought twenty false thumbs.

'So,' boomed the evil emperor the following week. 'Let's see the thumbs!'

So the scissor man emptied the false thumbs on to the floor. For one horrible moment, he thought the emperor was going to pick one up and examine it. But instead he said, 'Hmmm, well done, Scissor Man. Keep up the good work.'

And so, you see, the scissor man never had to cut off one thumb. If the emperor ever wanted to see the thumbs he had cut off, the scissor man just showed him the plastic ones!

The climbing lesson

Mother Monkey gathered her children round her at the foot of the tree. She was going to teach them to climb. Such a chattering they made as she showed them some nuts and berries. Then up the tree she climbed and placed the nuts and berries on a low overhanging branch.

There she sat calling to the little ones, urging them to climb. The eldest monkey tried once, then again. Each time he reached a little higher, until he climbed high enough.

Immediately he began to eat the food. The other monkeys were so worried that he might eat up the lot, they tried too. Eventually all except the youngest monkey were up in the tree eating nuts and berries.

Then Mother Monkey saw that the smallest monkey was still at the bottom squeaking sadly. Carefully she went down and gathered him in her arms. The food was gone, but Mother Monkey found some more.

'There you are, smallest monkey,' said Mother Monkey, 'that will make you very strong. Soon you'll be big enough to climb up all on your own.'

247

Snail hop

You will need:
a piece of chalk

This is a hopping game a bit like hopscotch, but you draw a coiled or snail shape to hop in, rather than a rectangle. This is how you play it.

Draw a snail shape on the ground with chalk. Mark it off in sections. Make them all different sizes. The game can be as hard as you want to make it, but each section must be big enough to fit one foot inside without touching the lines.

Now you can start. Take it in turns to hop on one foot from the start right round the coil to the centre of the 'snail'. You must hop in each section, and you are not allowed to touch any lines. If you do, you must go back and wait for your next turn. When you get to the centre you are allowed to rest on both feet. Then you must hop back to the start. You can use the other foot on the way back if you want to.

When you have hopped to the centre and back again, you may write your initials in one of the sections. It does not matter which one you write them in. This becomes your section and you are allowed to rest both feet in it for the rest of the game. All the other players have to hop over it.

The game is over when every section has some initials in it. The winner is the player with the most initialled sections.

A special prize

Janet decided that when she grew up she would be a jockey because she loved horses and ponies. She hadn't any of her own but Uncle Jack kept a pony specially for her on his farm.

Janet loved Snowball very much and every day after school she took some sugar lumps or carrots and went to feed her.

On Saturday mornings, Janet went up to Uncle Jack's very early, because he let her groom Snowball each week on Saturday. She stood on an upturned box and carefully brushed the pony until her coat was as smooth as silk.

'Janet,' said Uncle Jack one day, 'there's a pony show being held in the village next week. How about entering Snowball? There is a prize for the best kept pony and you certainly look after Snowball well.'

'What's the prize going to be?' asked Janet.

'I think it's a day at the races,' replied Uncle Jack. 'Now wouldn't you love to win that?'

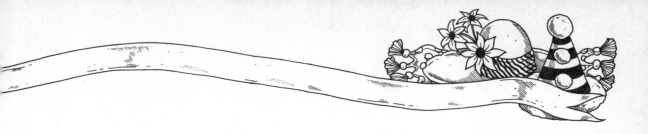

'Oh, yes, I would. What must I do to enter the show?' Janet said.

'I have a form which I will help you to fill in, but you had better ask Mummy and Daddy first,' said Uncle Jack.

Her mummy and daddy agreed that it was a lovely idea and Janet could hardly wait until the show day arrived. She spent all the week before grooming Snowball and Mummy gave her some brightly coloured streamers to hang from the pony's reins.

There were lots of ponies on show and the owners stood by nervously, waiting for the lady judge. She looked carefully at each pony and felt them all over. Janet held tightly on to Snowball waiting for their turn. The kind lady came at last and said, 'My, you have got a beauty there. I can see she has been very well cared for.'

Mummy, Daddy and Uncle Jack clapped loudly. 'Well done,' they told Janet as the judge fastened a big red rosette on to Snowball.

Janet, Mummy, Daddy and Uncle Jack spent a wonderful day at the races and Janet was even more certain that one day she would be a jockey.

Sir Tom

'Tom Thumb! Tom Thumb!' called the children as they ran around the school playground.

Tom was very small, but he didn't like being teased by the others. He wished he could suddenly grow a few centimetres. Then no one could call him Tom Thumb again.

The bell rang and everyone hurried back into school. Miss Green's lessons were always interesting and today she was talking about knights and castles in England long ago. 'I've got something exciting to tell you,' she said. 'Next week I am taking you on a trip to look round a castle. Then you will be able to see for yourselves the things we have been talking about this morning.'

It was a long drive to the castle, but at last the children tumbled out of the coach and followed Miss Green across the drawbridge and through the great stone entrance.

There was so much to see. They climbed a narrow, winding staircase to look out from the top of the tower. They shivered in the cold, dark dungeons and they looked down a deep well covered by an iron grating. 'Be careful you don't slip down through a hole in the grating, Tom,' laughed the children. 'You're small enough.'

At lunchtime the class picnicked on the bank of the moat and threw crumbs to the swans.

'Before we go home,' said Miss Green, 'we must look at the room where the armour and weapons are kept.'

The children thought this last room was the most exciting. There were huge swords and shields, axes and lances, and suits of shiny armour.

The guide showed them the different weapons. Finally he

said, 'And this is a suit of armour made for a child. Would one of you like to try it on?'

Everyone put up their hand, but the guide said, 'It'll have to be someone who isn't too big. How about you?' He pointed to Tom.

'Me? Yes, please,' said Tom. He stood in front of the class while the man helped him to buckle on the armour and when he tried to walk he squeaked and clanked horribly.

'Now you can see it properly,' said Miss Green. 'What a good thing Tom was here. No one else was the right size.'

Tom waved the small sword around his head.

'Sir Tom,' said the guide, which made everyone laugh. And from then on Tom was always known as Sir Tom, and he didn't mind that at all.

Garage

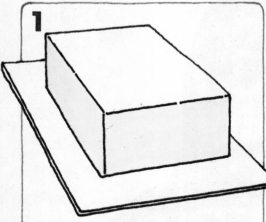

1

Turn the box upside down and paint it white all over. Paint one side of the large sheet of cardboard white too.

YOU WILL NEED
Small flat cardboard box
Piece of thick cardboard bigger than
    the base of the box
Smaller piece of thick card
4 or 5 matchboxes
Plain paper
String
Scissors
Sticky tape
Non-toxic glue
White emulsion paint and large
    brush
Your paint box, felt pens or crayons

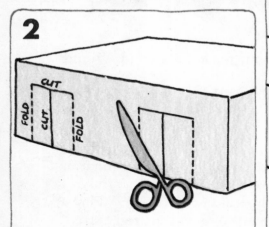

2

Ask a grown up to make cuts like this in one side of the box. Fold the flaps back carefully to make doors.

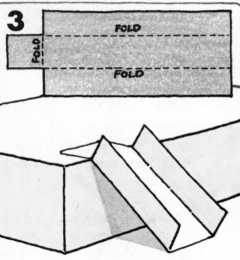

3

Make a ramp to lead to the garage roof from the cardboard, and tape it to the box. Stick the garage on to the large piece of cardboard which will be the forecourt.

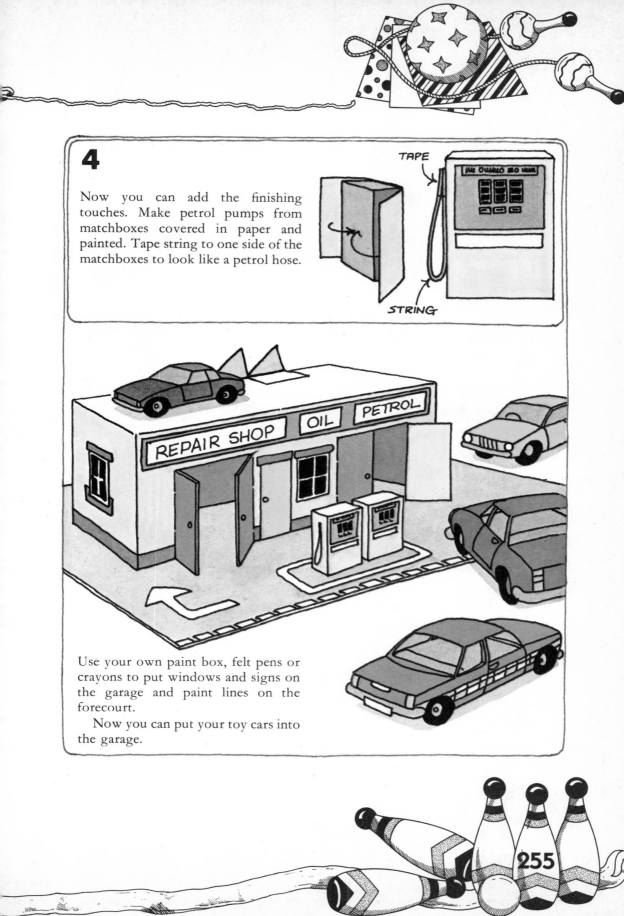

4

Now you can add the finishing touches. Make petrol pumps from matchboxes covered in paper and painted. Tape string to one side of the matchboxes to look like a petrol hose.

TAPE

STRING

REPAIR SHOP

OIL

PETROL

Use your own paint box, felt pens or crayons to put windows and signs on the garage and paint lines on the forecourt.

Now you can put your toy cars into the garage.

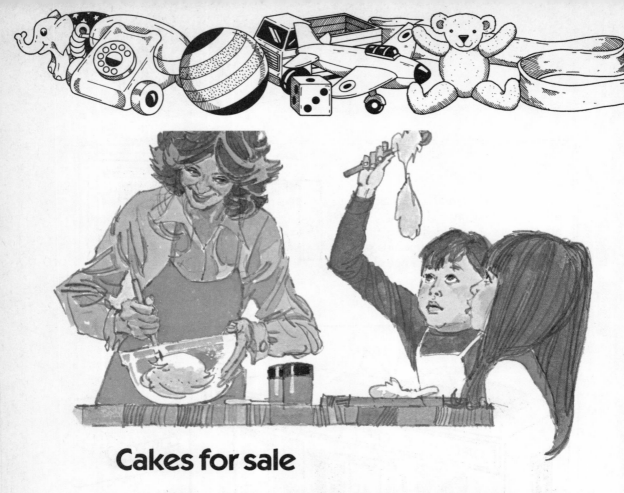

Cakes for sale

Mum was very busy making sausage rolls, tarts and buns to put in her freezer ready for Christmas. She mixed up the fat and flour, then rolled out the pastry on a floury board. When it was quite flat she cut out circles with a plastic cutter and pressed them into tins. Then she filled them with sticky red jam and popped them into the oven. They smelt delicious. Emma and Lawrence wanted to bake something too, but Mummy said she had far too much to do, to help them, so they would have to bake another day. Suddenly, she had an idea.

'Would you like to make some pretend cakes and have a cake shop?' she asked. Emma and Lawrence watched her mix up flour and water with lots of salt. 'The salt will stop the dough going bad,' Mummy explained, 'and you'll be able to play with your cakes for quite a while.'

When the dough was ready, the children put on their

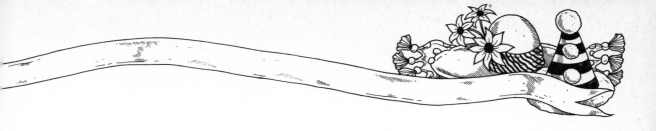

aprons and Mummy found them a space on the table. They
could manage all by themselves, and were soon patting and
rolling the dough into shapes. Emma made some fat
sausage shapes and put them on a baking tray in neat lines
of three. Lawrence made some of his dough into squashy
lumps. 'These are going to be rock buns,' he said.

They rolled out the left-over dough and borrowed a
cutter to make circles for the jam tarts. When the cakes and
buns were ready for baking, Mummy put them into the
oven. 'It will only take a few minutes,' she said, 'and when
they are cool you will be able to paint them.'

Emma and Lawrence had some orange squash and a
biscuit, and when their cakes were cool and hard, they took
their paints out. They painted yellow eclairs with brown
paint on top for chocolate. The buns they coloured brown,
with black dots for the currants. Emma's favourite cakes
were the jam tarts, yellow with bright red jam.

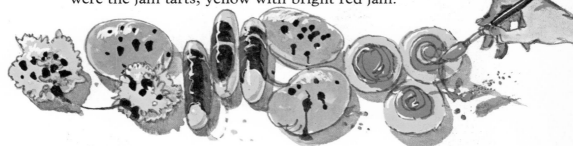

'My!' said Mum. 'They look good enough to eat.' She
sprayed the cakes with varnish and when they were dry,
Emma and Lawrence arranged them in boxes and wrote
out price tickets. They took turns at being the shop-keeper,
and when Dad came home they sold him four jam tarts and
an eclair.

'Don't forget to give them back when you've eaten them
Dad,' said Lawrence. 'We want to play shops again
tomorrow!'

Meera stops a thief

Meera the cow lived in Delhi. But she wasn't an ordinary cow – she was a *sacred* one, which meant that she could go where she pleased without anyone stopping her. She never had to learn the road-safety rules, because whenever she wanted to cross the road, all the traffic would stop for her.

Meera was very happy but sometimes she wished she could be of more use to the people of Delhi.

One day, as Meera was walking through the street market she saw a man steal a knife from a poor woman's stall.

'Stop, thief,' shouted the woman, but it was no use. The man had leapt on to his motorcycle and was roaring away.

This was Meera's chance. Quickly, she walked across the narrow street and lay down, completely blocking the way. The thief beeped his horn and shouted but Meera wouldn't budge.

A crowd of people surrounded the thief and the woman was given back her knife. She looked round for Meera in order to thank her, but, in all the commotion, Meera had slipped away, a big smile on her face. She had done something useful at last.

A wolf next door

Christopher was scared of wolves. At night, he thought they
were all round him. He thought that he could see their
long, thin bodies and hungry yellow eyes.

'It's just your imagination,' his mother told him.

One day, Christopher was playing near the garden hedge
when he heard a scuffling noise. He looked up. Poking
through the hedge was a brown, furry face, with slanting
eyes. A wolf!

Christopher ran. 'Mum,' he yelled. 'Mum, I saw a wolf.'

His mother calmed him down. 'We'll visit the new people
next door,' she said, 'and ask them.'

Mrs Davies, their new neighbour, was pleased to see them.
'I know what you saw,' she said. 'It was Robbie, our
Alsatian.'

A large animal came bounding into the room. 'It's a
wolf,' Christopher screamed.

Mrs Davies explained that Alsatian dogs did look a bit
like wolves. 'He's a very gentle dog,' she said.

Robbie licked Christopher and Christopher patted Robbie.
He was really a nice dog.

After that, Christopher often played with Robbie.
Sometimes, he pretended that Robbie was a wild wolf,
and that he had tamed him, all by himself.

Personal prints

You will need

Some large sheets of paper
Your paint box and brushes
Old plates you can mix paint on
Newspaper

This is a lovely way of making an unusual picture but it can be *very* messy so ask a grown-up for permission first!

Get yourself prepared by putting on something to cover your clothes and by putting lots of newspaper on the surfaces where you'll be printing. It's a good idea to have some tissues or a cloth and a bowl of water handy too, to clean yourself up between prints.

Mix up your paint and put it on a plate. It can be any colour but it must be nice and thick.

Put the palm of your hand down flat on to the plate and make sure it gets well covered with paint. Lift it off and press it down on to the paper. You can do the same with your other hand and with individual fingerprints too.

You can use your feet as well. This is a little more tricky – be careful not to stamp on the plate and break it! And you may have to paint your foot with a brush to make sure it's well covered, but you'll be left with some very interesting prints.

You can change the colours of the paint as often as you like so long as you wash your hands (or feet) in between each colour. Remember, too, to let one colour dry on the paper before adding another, or the colours will start to run into each other.

The sleepy tortoise

Bill the zoo keeper was very worried. His giant tortoise Stanley was *still* asleep!

'I hope he wakes up soon,' said Bill to all the children, one spring day. 'It will be his birthday soon. I hope he won't sleep for ever and ever. He's very old is Stanley. Very, very big and very, very old. He's older than all you children. He's older than me. And he's older than my grandad. He'll be a hundred years old on his next birthday – if he wakes up.' And Bill looked more worried than ever.

Stanley liked living at the zoo because people were very kind to him and sometimes gave him treats – like strawberries and yellow dandelion flowers to eat. But every autumn when the weather got colder, he would go into the corner of his pen and burrow into the soil and go fast asleep until the warm spring weather came back again. But this year Stanley stayed asleep even when the warm spring weather came.

One day, Bill said sadly to the children, 'It will be Stanley's birthday on Saturday – but I'm afraid he won't be awake in time.'

Then suddenly one of the children shouted, 'Stanley's waking up!' And slowly, very slowly, the earth in the corner of the pen began to move. And slowly, very slowly, Stanley's shell appeared. And slowly, very slowly, his head came out from the shell and he opened his eyes.

'He must have heard us!' gasped Bill. 'He doesn't want to miss his party after all.'

Bill was so delighted that he rushed away and came back with a big cabbage for Stanley to eat and quickly, very quickly, Stanley ripped off the green spring leaves with his huge jaws and crunched them up.

'He's woken up properly at last!' said everyone. And they were so pleased, they all came to Stanley's one hundredth birthday party and brought their own little pet tortoises too.

263

James stops a thief

James wanted to be a detective when he grew up. One day he found a strange man's footstep in the flowerbed. He looked at it through his magnifying glass. 'It's not Dad's footprint, and I know it isn't the milkman's. That means it must be a thief's.

He crept into the house, opened the sitting-room door and peered in. There was the burglar, about to steal the television! Quickly, James fetched some rope. Then he crept up behind the burglar, who was bending over to unplug the television, and wound the rope round his chest and arms.

'AHHHHH!' cried the burglar. 'What are you doing?'

'I'm tying you up and then I'm going to ring the police,' said James, busily tying strong knots.

'But . . .' began the burglar.

'Save all your talking for when the police arrive,' said James.

And then his mother, who'd heard the noise, came rushing in. 'James, what *are* you doing?' she asked.

'I've just caught a burglar, Mum,' said James proudly.

'But that's not a burglar,' she said, horrified. 'That's the man who's come to mend our television.'

James turned white. 'Oh – I'm terribly sorry,' he said, quickly untying the knots. But the TV repair man saw the funny side – once he'd been untied.

The dream

Lisa was having a lovely time. She was riding very fast in a great big car down a beautiful glittery avenue. The trees on either side were like willow trees, only the leaves were silver, and from each branch hung a big, sticky bun. As the car sped along, Lisa reached out her hand and, with no trouble at all, picked one of the buns from a tree.

A gruff voice beside her said, 'A pretty nice place this, isn't it?'

She looked down and there beside her on the seat sat her cat Blinkers, smiling up at her and cleaning his whiskers. He had just eaten a big, sticky bun too.

'Oh look,' said Blinkers, and pointed his paw ahead. There in front of them lay a shimmering lake surrounded by the silver trees.

'Goodness,' said Lisa, as the car wove between the trees, 'we're going to go straight in.'

'Wake up darling. It's time to get dressed for school,' said a voice from a long way off. Lisa stretched and yawned.

'Oh Mummy, I've had such a lovely, exciting dream,' she said. She felt a weight on her leg. It was Blinkers. He stretched and yawned too, and for a moment she almost thought he winked at her.

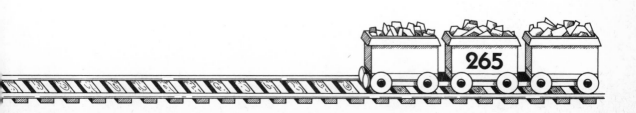

Artist

You will need:
a felt-tipped pen
a sheet of paper
a blindfold (a scarf or piece of cloth).

This is a very funny game. With help from a grown-up, pin a big sheet of blank paper on the wall.

One person is chosen to be the artist. Put the blindfold on him and give him the pen. Then ask him to draw the main shape of a house or other object. The other children now take it in turns to ask him to add things to the picture, such as a door, windows, a chimney, a garden and people. Unless the artist is extremely clever, his drawing will probably look very messy and funny, and nothing like a house!

Red rover all over

The more players you have for this the better. Everyone lines up on one side in the garden or in a big playroom if you have one. Choose one person to stand alone, some distance away from the line.

When he shouts 'Red Rover all over', everyone must run over to the other side of the garden or room. The person who stands on his own tries to catch one of the others as they run past him. Whoever is caught stands with him as the children run back the other way. Together they try and catch more people. The game continues until there is one person left to be caught. He is the winner.

The lost ball

There once lived a little girl, Kay, who had a brown dog called Bertie. One morning, Kay said, 'Happy Birthday, Bertie. Did you know it's your special day today?'

'Woof!' said Bertie, and he wagged his tail.

'Look what I've got for you,' said Kay. And she opened a paper bag and brought out – a big yellow ball.

'Woof-woof!' said Bertie, and his tail wagged faster than ever.

'After breakfast, we'll go for a walk in the field and play with your new ball,' Kay said. And so they did.

For a while they played throw-and-catch. Then Kay decided it was time for hide-and-seek. So while Bertie lay down on the grass, the little girl hid the ball behind a tree nearby. 'Find it, Bertie!' she said. And he did.

Then it was Bertie's turn. He carried the ball in his mouth looking for a good place to hide it. Among the roots of the tree was a dark hole. That would make a good hiding place! Bertie dropped the yellow ball into the hole. But – oh dear! – it rolled right out of sight. 'Woof!' barked Bertie loudly. 'Woof-woof!'

Kay came running up. 'Oh Bertie, where's your ball?' she asked. Then she saw the hole. 'Naughty dog, have you lost it down that rabbit hole? Now we won't be able to get it out again.'

268

And she was right – they couldn't. They had to leave the yellow ball behind. And that evening when her father came home, the little girl told him what had happened.

'Don't worry, Kay,' he said. 'I know how we can get the ball back.' After tea, Kay's father looked in a cupboard and found an old walking stick.

When they reached the spot where the rabbit hole was, Kay's father pushed the curly handle of the walking stick into the hole.

'What are you doing?' cried Kay.

'Wait and see,' said her father. When the walking stick was a little way down the hole he began to pull it out again, very carefully. And there, hooked inside the curly handle, was Bertie's yellow ball!

'Woof-woof!' barked Bertie happily, wagging his rail.

'Fetch it!' cried Kay, and she threw the ball high into the air. Bertie chased after it, and when he caught it he carried it in his mouth all the way home and put it in his basket.

After that he took the greatest care not to lose his yellow ball again.

The naughty zebra

The children were happy because Grandad was taking them to the zoo. He bought a lollipop each for the children to enjoy as they walked around. Soon after that they came to the zebra enclosure.

Simon liked the zebras because their stripes reminded him of his pyjamas.

The children had a favourite zebra who always stood by the fence to greet visitors.

'Look, here's your zebra coming to see us,' said Grandad. 'I think she is getting to know you two.' Simon patted her head while Sarah licked her lollipop. Suddenly Sarah felt the zebra nibbling gently at her tee shirt. She turned round and before she knew what was happening the zebra put her head over the bar and knocked the lollipop out of her hand.

'You naughty zebra,' Sarah said and started to cry.

'I think it's the zebras' feeding time,' laughed Grandad.

Sarah dried her tears and went back to the shop to buy another lollipop, but this time she held it very tightly indeed!

270

The leprechaun

In Ireland, nestled where the mountains sweep down towards the sea, lay a group of tiny, white cottages.

Bronagh lived here. She was a little girl with eyes as green and beautiful as the land around her. One day she was searching the hillside for a shamrock, for tomorrow was St Patrick's Day, and to wear a shamrock then was very lucky. But she couldn't find one anywhere. She flopped on the grass and sighed.

'Help!' squeaked a voice. 'You're sitting on me!' Bronagh jumped up. She saw a little tiny man dressed all in green. 'A leprechaun!' she gasped.

He nodded. 'And my foot is caught on a root,' he squeaked. 'If you free me, you can have a share of my crock of gold!'

Bronagh pulled the roots and freed him. 'I don't want your fairy-gold,' she said, 'but I do want a shamrock, so I can wear it tomorrow.'

The leprechaun pointed to a crooked tree. 'You'll find your shamrock under there, now and every year. But never tell, or it will not grow again.' Then he was gone.

And for ever after, people wondered how Bronagh always had a lucky shamrock to wear on St Patrick's Day.

A black cat

Snowflake was a beautiful, silky-haired white cat. She was rather fat and had large green eyes and very long hair, and she lived with a little girl called Katy and her parents in a little cottage in the country.

One evening Katy was worried because Snowflake didn't come when she called her.

'Don't worry Katy,' said Daddy. 'I'll look for Snowflake after you've gone to bed. She can't have gone far because it's chilly outside.'

Daddy went outside later with his torch and called, 'Snowflake! Snowflake!'

It was very cold outside and the wind was howling. He hugged his coat round him and went back inside.

'No sign of her,' he said to Katy's mother.

'Oh dear,' Mummy replied. 'I hope she hasn't got lost.'

Katy was very sad the next morning when she discovered Snowflake hadn't returned, and even sadder the following day when there was still no sign of her cat.

The next day the coalman called. He was big and tall with

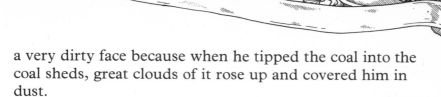

a very dirty face because when he tipped the coal into the coal sheds, great clouds of it rose up and covered him in dust.

'Good morning,' he said to Katy's mother. 'Where do I put the coal?'

'Thank goodness you've come,' she replied. 'We ran out of coal a week ago, and it's got so cold. Katy – you show the coalman where to put the coal.'

Katy led the coalman round to the back of the house to the coal shed. The coalman opened the little door and peered in. At that moment there was a loud 'miaow!'

'Bless my soul!' said the coalman.

'Snowflake!' said Katy.

Out ran a little black cat.

'Oh,' Katy said in disappointment. 'It's not Snowflake at all. It's a black cat. Still, it looks very hungry so I'll take it in and give it some milk.'

The cat purred a great deal when Katy picked her up and took her indoors.

'I've found a black cat in the coal shed, Mummy,' said Katy.

Mummy took a look at the purring cat and laughed. 'Silly,' she said. 'It's Snowflake!' She picked up an old cloth and rubbed it on the cat's back. 'Look!' she cried. 'She's all covered in soot – that's why she looks black. She must have got shut in the coal shed and as we ran out of coal we haven't been in there for a few days.'

Paper plate flower

1

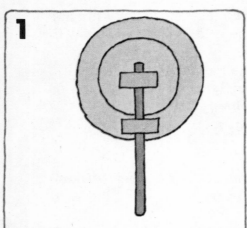

Tape a thin stick to the flat side of a paper plate.

2

You can make a very simple flower by just painting a flower on to the plate.

3

If you want to make a more detailed flower, cut out lots of different coloured petal shapes from tissue or crepe paper.

4

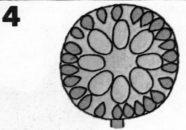

Tape or glue these petals to the paper plate. Stick them round the rim first and then work inwards.

5

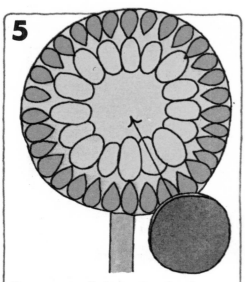

Cut out a small circle of card and cover it with coloured paper and stick it in the centre of the flower.

6

You can make magic flowers with petals of all different colours or you can make flowers that look like the flowers in your garden.

Cutting out all the petals separately can take time, so if you are in a hurry here's a quick way to make them.

7

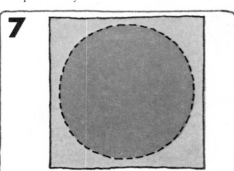

Cut out a square of tissue or crepe paper a little bigger than your paper plate.

8

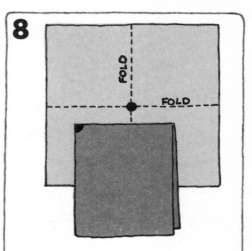

FOLD

FOLD

Fold the square into four, marking the centre.

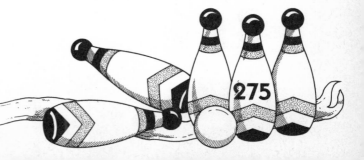

275

9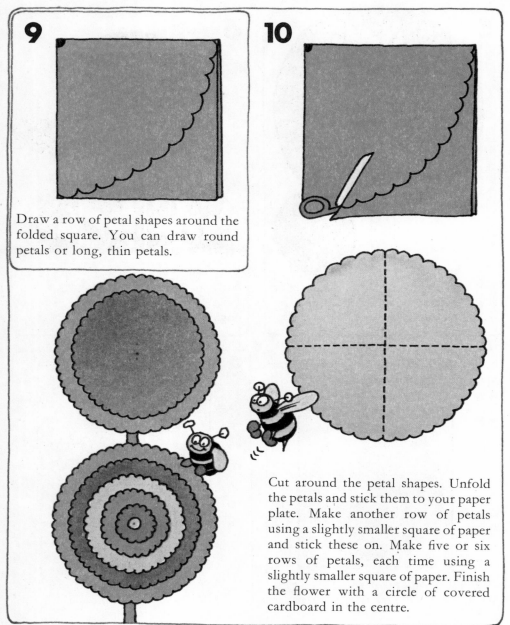

Draw a row of petal shapes around the folded square. You can draw round petals or long, thin petals.

10

Cut around the petal shapes. Unfold the petals and stick them to your paper plate. Make another row of petals using a slightly smaller square of paper and stick these on. Make five or six rows of petals, each time using a slightly smaller square of paper. Finish the flower with a circle of covered cardboard in the centre.

Lollipop tree

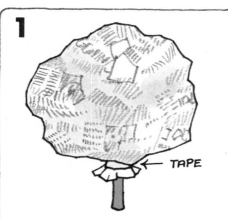

1

TAPE

Crumple a few sheets of newspaper into a ball. Push a thin stick into the ball of newspaper and hold it in place with sticky tape.

YOU WILL NEED
Tin foil
Old newspaper
Yoghurt pot
Earth or sand
Thin stick
Scraps of plain and coloured paper
Scissors
Sticky tape
Non-toxic glue
Your paint box, felt pens or crayons

3

Cover the yoghurt pot with foil and fill it with earth or sand. Push the stick into the sand.

2

Cover the newspaper ball in tin foil.

Now you can decorate the tree. You could make it into a fruit tree – sticking on apples or oranges you have cut out and painted – or you could have a flowery tree. Cut out and colour paper flowers then stick them to the tree.

277

Theresa's picnic

Theresa was excited because today all the families from the farms in the Spanish valley where she lived would climb the hill for the grand picnic.

Theresa collected a bundle of sticks, her mother packed a big basket of food and her father carried it all up the hill.

In a shady spot Father lit the fire while Mother unpacked the rice and fish and chicken and vegetables to make paella.

Suddenly Mother exclaimed, 'I've forgotten the cooking pot. What shall we do!'

Just then a hat came rolling past. Theresa caught it. 'I'll go and see whose hat this is,' she said.

Further up the path an old man and his wife were sitting by a cooking pot. 'You've found my hat,' said the old man. 'Many thanks. Are you enjoying the picnic?'

Theresa told them about the cooking pot.

'Please use ours,' said the old lady. 'Our soup is almost ready.'

Mother was delighted to see the cooking pot. 'Would those kind people like to picnic with us?' she said. Theresa hurried back to invite them.

When the meal was over, the old man played folksongs on his guitar and everyone gathered around their fire and sang and danced until nightfall.

278

The new curtains

Jenny was ill. She lay in bed and stared at her curtains. They were old and worn and drab, and flapped wearily against the window. Jenny found them dull to look at but was too ill to sit up and read.

Mummy came in and looked at Jenny anxiously. She saw her staring at the dowdy curtains and had an idea. 'I'll go out right away Jenny, and buy a length of pretty material and make you some bright new curtains to look at.'

Mummy worked hard, and by tea-time the curtains were finished and hung up. All that week Jenny lay quietly, watching the pictures on her new curtains.

The curtains were green and blue and had flowers and animals and birds in orange, red and yellow. There were tall reeds to one side and a flock of geese flying over a cool blue lake. They were so nice that she was sure they helped her to get better.

Baa, baa, black sheep

Baa, baa, black sheep,
Have you any wool?

Yes Sir, yes Sir,
Three bags full.

One for my master,
And one for my dame.

And one for the little boy
Who lives down the lane.

Little Tommy Tucker

Little Tommy Tucker
Sang for his supper.
What shall we give him?
Brown bread and butter.
How will he cut it
Without a knife?
How can he marry
Without e'er a wife?

Humpty Dumpty

Humpty Dumpty sat on the wall,
Humpty Dumpty had a great fall.
All the king's horses and all the king's men,
Couldn't put Humpty together again!

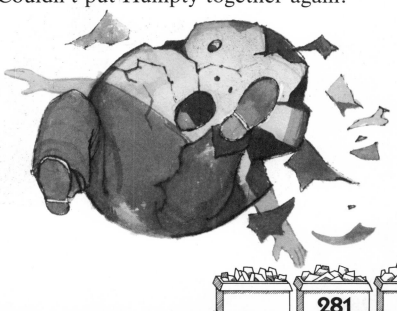

Your own newspaper

You will need

Some large sheets of paper
Biro and felt pens
Stapler

Why not make your own newspaper all about yourself, your friends, and your family?

All you need to do is fold up some large sheets of paper and put them inside each other. (Staple them together if you've got a stapler.)

Now think of a front page headline – it can be anything that's happened recently. 'John Starts New School' perhaps, or 'Mum Scores a Goal'. Then write underneath John's feelings about his new school and what happened on his first day, or interview Mum and ask how she came to score a goal in the family football match – had she been in training long beforehand? Don't forget to draw pictures of the events too!

Add all the other bits of news you can think of to make your paper interesting reading. You could have a fashion page with a sketch of the jeans and shirt your brother bought recently. Put in a recipe – choose your favourite, someone might take the hint and make it for you!

You could write a review of a television programme you've seen recently or recommend a programme that's going to be on soon. Look at a real newspaper for lots more ideas.

Your family and friends will love reading about themselves – they've probably always wanted to see their names in the newspaper!

The bicycle ride

One day, Dad came home from work with a strange bicycle. 'It's a tandem,' he said. 'It's a bicycle made for two.'

'But we need a bicycle made for five, Dad,' said Poppy, 'because there's me and Mum and Toby and Tina as well.'

'There's a sidecar for Toby and Tina to sit in,' said Mum, 'and there's a seat on the back for you, Poppy.'

So one sunny spring day they all set off on the tandem for a ride into the country.

Dad sat in front and pedalled. Mum sat behind him and pedalled. Poppy sat on the seat behind Mum and the twins sat in the sidecar. The twins and Poppy waved to everyone they passed.

After a while they came to a hill and Dad began to puff and pant and he said to Mum, 'Are you pedalling?'

'Yes, I am!' puffed Mum. 'I'm pedalling as hard as I can.'

Then Dad said, 'Stop. We must all get off and push. This hill is too steep.'

'Are we in the countryside yet, Mum?' asked Poppy as she pushed the tandem along.

'Nearly,' gasped Mum. 'It's over the top of this hill.'

When they reached the top of the hill they saw all the countryside spread out – with trees and fields and a river

and a farm. Then they all got on the tandem again and whizzed down the hill towards the river.

'No need to pedal, now,' laughed Dad.

But just as they got near the river something happened. The tandem went all wobbly and jolty and the wheels slowed down and went wooomp-plonk, wooomp-plonk, wooomp-plonk and Poppy began to go wooomp-plonk too.

'Off we get,' said Dad. 'We must have hit a sharp stone. The back tyre's burst. We've got a puncture and we can't go on until it's mended.'

Then, just when everyone was struggling away with spanners and bicycle inner tubes and repair kits, a bus stopped by the river and lots of people got out to have a picnic.

'What's up, mate?' said the bus driver to Dad.

'A puncture,' said Dad.

'We'll soon fix it,' said the bus driver as he helped Mum and Dad. And all the passengers shared their big picnic with Mum, Dad, Poppy and the twins.

The wind

The wind in spring is a busy wind. It has to blow away all the old bits and pieces that belong to winter and make the land ready for spring. It isn't a cold wind, for it needs to warm the ground, but it isn't a soft wind either. It is very strong. It wakes everything up.

First the busy wind blows into the woods, scattering last year's dead leaves and pushing them to one side. It unblocks the holes where the creatures are hiding. 'Come out. Get about. Spring is here,' it calls down their holes.

Then it blows hard against the trees, tugging angrily at the old brown leaves left clinging to the branches. It breaks off small dead twigs for the birds to pick up to build their new nests. 'Stop resting. Get nesting,' it calls to the birds.

Next the warm wind blows over the fields, melting the last patches of winter snow. As it blows it calls down to the seeds, 'Start to grow. There's no more snow.'

Finally, when the spring wind is satisfied it has completed its work, it blows itself right away.

The attic dragon

Graham lay in bed, wide awake and very frightened. He could hear strange noises above him in the attic, and they seemed to be getting louder.

At first he had thought that it was a rat that was gnawing through the ceiling and would land – plop! – on his pillow at any moment. Then he thought it was a monster getting crosser and crosser because it had been locked in the attic and would soon start to roar and howl with rage. Or, maybe it was a giant, who'd make the whole house shake. Or maybe, thought Graham, really frightened now, it was a dragon who was planning to set the house on fire!

Graham couldn't stand it any longer. He jumped out of bed and ran downstairs to his parents, who were watching television.

'There's a dragon in the attic,' cried Graham. 'I think it's going to set the house on fire.'

'We'll go and have a look, shall we?' said Graham's mother.

So they went upstairs and she opened the attic door. There was a flash of ginger fur, and the 'dragon' had vanished down the stairs.

Graham's mother laughed. 'Your "dragon" was none other than Marmalade, the cat. I must have shut him in the attic by mistake when I was up there earlier on.'

Graham laughed. How very relieved he felt!

Simon says

Choose one player to stand out in front of the group. He tells you what to do. You must obey him whenever he says something that starts with 'Simon says'. If he calls 'Simon says pat your head', you pat your head. If he calls 'Simon says circle your arms like a windmill', you circle your arms like a windmill. But if he gives you an order without the 'Simon says' you must stand quite still. If you move the tiniest bit you are out. The one to stay in the longest is the winner. She becomes the next Simon.

288

Circle ball

You will need:
a ball
a long string
a piece of cloth or net

Play this with a number of people. Find a large ball and tie it to a long string. The best way to do this is to wrap the ball in cloth or a piece of net, and tie the string to that.

Players stand in a large circle. One person stands in the middle of the circle and swings the ball around on the end of the string. The players have to jump over the ball as it swings around.

As soon as a player is touched by the ball, she is out. The last one to be out is the winner.

Vera's surprise

Vera was very lonely. She wouldn't play with her friends any more because they always went to the woods to chase squirrels and birds.

'Cheer up,' said Mummy. 'Marie is coming for lunch. She will tell you about her new job with Mr James, the vet.'

Although Marie was older than Vera, they always enjoyed talking to each other. After lunch, Marie waited for Mr James to collect her because they had to go and treat some sick animals.

When Mr James arrived Marie told him that Vera's friends chased animals in the woods and left Vera at home.

'Well, why don't you come with us Vera, if your mother doesn't mind?' Mr James suggested.

'Oh super,' said Vera excitedly. Soon she was sitting in Mr James's car next to his dog, Bimbo.

They went to a small village where Vera watched the vet change the bandage on a little dog's leg. The dog had broken its leg but it was now almost better. They called at two farms and Vera played in the fields with Bimbo while the vet looked at some cows and horses. One of the farmers gave Vera a ride on his horse.

As they arrived home, Vera was surprised to see her friends waiting for her.

'Vera has told me you've all been chasing animals,' Mr James said to them crossly.

Bobby, the eldest, said to Mr James, 'No we haven't. We were going to, but then we remembered Vera saying it was cruel and we decided not to chase them ever again.'

'I am glad to hear that,' said Mr James smiling. 'Look, I'd like to show you all what fun it is to be kind to animals. If you all bring some lunch and come along to the kennels tomorrow, you can help me for the day. I've got lots of work to do and there are twenty-two dogs that need to be brushed and taken for walks.'

'Oh, smashing,' shouted Bobby excitedly.

'Thank you,' shouted the others.

'Don't thank me,' said Mr James. 'You should thank Vera. She was sensible enough to stay at home and not go with you to frighten the animals. If she had gone, I wouldn't have met any of you.'

'We're sorry to have been nasty, Vera,' said Bobby.

'That's all right,' said Vera, who was glad to be with her friends again. 'Let's decide what food to take tomorrow. It will be a lovely day out.'

A swimming lesson

Mummy had promised Elspeth and Daisy that they could join a swimming club and the twins were very proud of their new red swimming costumes. She had also bought them some rubber water wings which would help them to keep afloat while they were learning to swim.

Mrs Jones who was to be their teacher said that they must walk carefully alongside the big bath until they came to the learners' pool. The girls carried their costumes wrapped up in big, bright towels.

'Here are the changing rooms,' Mrs Jones told them. 'Get changed, put your water wings on and come to the side of the pool.'

Soon they were ready and Mummy had changed into her yellow swimming costume too. They had changed very quickly because they were so eager to learn to swim.

Mrs Jones was standing ready for them, but first she suggested that they walk through the shower. Then, Mummy wrapped them in their towels and they listened carefully to their teacher. The other children listened too as she explained that they could first splash about in the shallow end of the pool, just to get used to the water.

'The water smells very funny,' said Elspeth.

'Yes,' said Mrs Jones, 'that's because it has chlorine in it.'

'What is the chlorine for?' asked Daisy.

'It helps to keep the water clean, so that we don't pick up any germs while swimming. You will soon get used to the smell and you won't notice it after a while,' Mrs Jones told them.

The twins loved splashing about in the pool but soon the teacher blew her whistle and called them to one side.

'Children, I want you to hold on tightly to this rail and then move your legs like this.' She climbed into the water to show them what they must do.

The twins soon managed to kick their legs properly.

'Next week I will teach you how to use your arms,' Mrs Jones told them. 'That's all for this time.'

Everyone had enjoyed themselves so much that they didn't want to come out of the water. The twins said that they wished the lesson could have lasted longer.

'Never mind,' said Mummy, 'you can have another lesson soon. Let's get dressed and we will go to the café.' The twins had enjoyed their first swimming lesson.

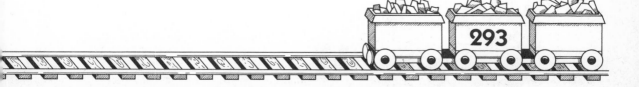

Matchstick puzzle

You will need

12 matchsticks

Arrange the 12 matches in four squares like this.

Now ask your friend if she can change the pattern to leave only three squares, by moving only three of the matches.

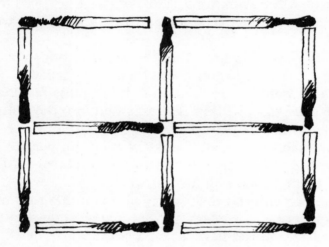

Here is the answer so you can practise in advance.

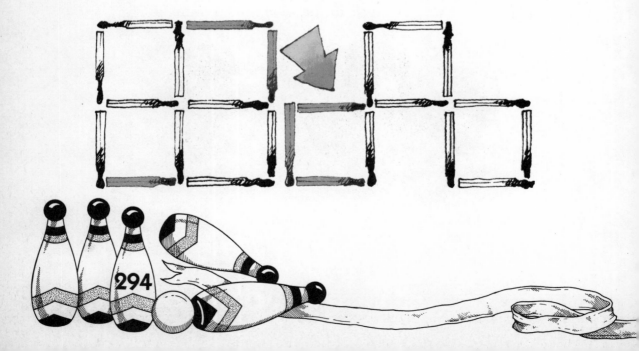

294

Flip cartoon

You will need

A small note pad
Your crayons or felt pens

This is a very easy way to make a cartoon which really seems to move.

1 Take the first page of a small notepad and draw a simple figure.

2 Then on the second page of the notepad, in exactly the same position on the page, draw the same figure but with a slight difference.

3 Now hold the notepad up so that the picture is facing you. Take hold of the corner of the page, flip the page backwards and forwards and watch your picture move!

Here is another idea for a flip cartoon.

Martin's model

Martin had a model aeroplane kit and Daddy opened the box and read the instructions. 'Let's see,' he said. 'These letters marked on the pieces of wood are to tell us which parts to stick together. We must be careful to get it right.'

'This large piece must be the body,' said Martin, 'and these look like wing shapes.'

'You are quite right,' Daddy told him. 'Find the tail piece, Martin, read out what is on the paper and then we can start.'

Martin was thrilled to see the aeroplane taking shape and soon it was finished.

'Let's try it out in the garden,' said Daddy.

They went outside and Martin was so excited. 'It flies, it flies!' he shouted.

They played for an hour with it and then a sad thing happened. A gust of wind carried the aeroplane up into a tall tree.

'Oh dear,' said Martin, nearly in tears. 'How can we get it back?'

It had stuck in the thickest branches. Luckily the window cleaner was on his ladder and he had seen what had happened. 'Don't worry,' he said kindly, 'I will get it for you. I'll bring my ladder round.'

Martin was so glad when he had his aeroplane back.

296

Not playing

One day, Tony's mother sent him out to play when he just didn't feel like playing. 'You don't want to be inside on a nice day like this,' she said. 'Run out and play.'

Tony went out but he did not play. 'She can't make me play,' he said to himself. 'I don't feel like it.'

So, he tried to think of things to do that were not playing.

He kicked stones until the toes of his black shoes became grey. He found some ants and watched where they came from, where they were going and what they were carrying. He took a hammer from the garage, found a stone and banged it with the hammer until it cracked. He turned on the garden hose and made a river on the path. He chased the cat until it scampered up the birch tree. He climbed on to the coal bunker and fróm there to the garage roof. It was sloping and it scared him.

When he had done all these things that were not playing, he went to the kitchen door. 'Can I come in now?' he asked. 'Of course,' said his mother. 'You have had a good play.'

Orange picking

The old town of Jaffa is in Israel. Jaffa has mosques, dome-roofed houses and some of the narrowest of streets and stairways. Near the town are many orange groves.

One holidaytime, Nurit gathered her brothers and sisters around her. 'Soon,' she said, 'it will be Grandfather's birthday. I think we should buy him a new hookah pipe.'

'With what?' asked David, her eldest brother. 'We haven't any money.'

'I know,' nodded Nurit. 'But there are six of us, and between us we should be able to earn enough.'

'Me earn,' said Rachel, her baby sister.

David looked at her in dismay. 'But what can we do which includes the little ones?'

'We will work in the orange groves!' answered Nurit. So they walked, in a line, through Jaffa, and down to the orange groves. There, they were given wooden buckets to put the oranges in. The man laughed at them, saying, 'I can't see you children gathering many.'

But they tried. They filled the buckets, then emptied them into a large, wooden crate. At the end of an hour, they were hot, thirsty, and nowhere near to filling one crate. Rachel

had given up long ago, and was sitting down sucking an orange.

'This won't do,' sighed Nurit. 'The buckets are too heavy.'

Then she had an idea, and, as they rested awhile, she explained her plan to her brothers and sisters.

When they began picking again, the man stared in astonishment. For the children were in a line, from the orange trees to the crate, and not using a bucket at all! Nurit picked an orange, then it was passed right down the line to Rachel, who popped it into the crate with glee.

Soon, they had filled enough crates for the money they needed.

They all ran back to Jaffa, to the street market, which sells everything you can think of. The children had a lovely time wandering around and choosing a hookah pipe for their grandfather. When they had bought it, they found that they had a little money left over. Enough to buy a large glass of 'mitz' each, which is – fresh orange-juice!

Tin can totem pole

YOU WILL NEED
Lots of tin cans with reusable lids
Sheets of plain paper
Scraps of thin card
Egg boxes
Sticky tape
Non-toxic glue
Your paint box, felt pens or crayons

1

TAPE

EGG BOX

Make sure the lids are firmly on the tins, then wrap paper around each tin and fasten it with sticky tape. Now you can paint on totem pole faces. Stick on noses, beaks and ears made from cardboard – or from egg boxes.

2

Pile the tins up, putting the biggest at the bottom.

Making a tin can totem pole is extra fun if you get all your friends to bring a tin. Then each of you can decorate your own tin and you can see who can make the most frightening face.

300

Jam jar snowstorm

YOU WILL NEED
Small screw top jar
Small plastic model
Glycerin (can be bought at any
    chemist)
Glitter
Non-toxic waterproof glue
Water
Teaspoon

1

LID

If the jar still has a label on it soak it off. Make sure the inside of the lid is clean and dry and stick a small plastic model to it. The little figures sold as cake decorations are ideal or use a small plastic toy. Make sure the model will fit inside the jar.

3

Make sure the model is stuck firmly to the lid, then screw the lid firmly on the jar. Turn the jar upside down and shake well. The glittery 'snow' will fall around the figure inside.

2

Fill the jar two-thirds full with glycerin. Top it up with water and stir in teaspoonful of glitter.

Martin at school

Miss Timmins's nursery class was the happiest in the whole school, or it was until Martin arrived.

Most children love school, but not Martin. He cried and screamed every day. 'I want to go home,' he shouted, until poor Miss Timmins didn't know what to do.

One morning Miss Timmins was giving out the milk when she came to Martin's place and saw that he had gone. She looked everywhere. At last she reached the kitchen, and there was Martin sitting on a table with a cake in his hand.

'Here I am,' he cried, waving the cake. 'You didn't tell me my Aunty Rose was here.'

Aunty Rose was the school cook, and she was very sorry when she heard how naughty Martin had been.

'You must go back to your teacher at once,' she said.

'No, I want to stay here,' he shouted. 'I want . . .'

'Martin, that's enough,' interrupted Aunty sternly.

'Now listen,' said Miss Timmins. 'If you promise to come back to the classroom quietly, then you may see your Aunty every playtime this week.'

So Martin promised, and began to enjoy coming to school.

After three days he said, 'I can't come tomorrow Aunty. I'm too busy helping teacher. I have to feed the goldfish every playtime now. Do you mind?'

'Of course not,' said Aunty Rose smiling. 'I understand.'

302

The shopping list

There was once a pencil who was tired of writing Mr Brown's boring old shopping list every day. He didn't want to write shopping lists – he wanted to write stories!

One day, when Mr Brown was out of the room, the pencil decided to change the shopping list around, just a little.

Later that day, Mr Brown put the shopping list and the pencil in a basket and went to Mrs Peabody's corner shop. There he read out what he thought was the shopping list, his eyes growing rounder and rounder with surprise. This is what he read:

'Once upon a time there were some magic jam tarts, who decided to hold a dance. They waved their magic wands, and up leapt the packet of frozen peas, the carton of milk and the pork chop. The six eggs started to tap dance, the lettuce and packet of tea did the twist, the pork sausages jived with four bananas, while the tin of cat food waltzed with the tin of beans.'

'Well,' said Mrs Peabody, laughing. 'That's the strangest shopping list I ever heard.'

'I wonder who could have written it?' said Mr Brown. 'It certainly wasn't me, and yet the funny thing is, it's written in my handwriting.'

No one noticed the pencil in the basket. He was laughing so much that his wooden sides almost split!

303

The baby goldfish

Luke lived in the middle of a great big city, but he was luckier than a lot of his friends, for his house had a garden and, best of all, in the garden was a fishpond which had at least ten goldfish in it.

Luke fed the goldfish every Saturday with some food he bought from Mrs Salmon's pet shop.

'Now, only feed them once a week, Luke,' Mrs Salmon had told him. 'The rest of the time they can eat the insects that float on the surface of the water. Goldfish are nearly always hungry and will eat everything you give them, and fat goldfish aren't healthy.'

Every Saturday, the goldfish were waiting for Luke. It was almost as if they counted off the days of the week on their fins, Luke thought to himself with a smile. They hovered near the surface with their mouths open, while Luke sprinkled the food about like pepper.

They were very greedy goldfish and, with a few large gulps, all the food was gone!

One late spring day, Luke was cleaning out some paper which had blown into the pond when he noticed a very tiny dark fish swimming under a water lily. He looked more closely at the water and saw that there was not one but at least twenty little fish swimming around. He couldn't understand how they had got there.

He ran in to ask his mum but she couldn't understand it either. So they looked up 'goldfish' in a big book and discovered that baby goldfish often had dark scales when they were young, but would gradually become gold as they got older.

Luke was thrilled to know they had baby goldfish, and every day he would examine the little fish to see if they were

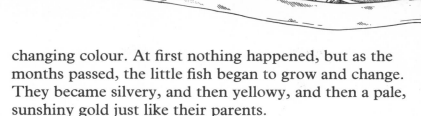

changing colour. At first nothing happened, but as the months passed, the little fish began to grow and change. They became silvery, and then yellowy, and then a pale, sunshiny gold just like their parents.

But Luke saw that two of the babies never did quite manage to become completely gold – they remained silvery with a few gold scales and were very pretty and less shy than the others and would often come to the surface of the water and blink at him. They were his favourites and he always gave them just a little bit extra to eat.

Long jump

You will need an even number of players for this jumping
game. Any number between ten and twenty will do. Divide
into two equal teams and choose a leader for each. Line up
behind them at the start.

Each leader makes a standing jump from the start. The next
team member jumps from where the leader landed, and so on
down the line until the last player has her turn.

Now measure the distances jumped. The team which jumps
the furthest wins.

306

Under and over ball

You will need:
a ball

Make up two teams of about six players each. Line up behind each other with spaces between you. Stand with legs apart.

The first person in each team bends down and tosses the ball backwards between his legs to the next player. She catches it and tosses it over her head to the player behind her. He in his turn tosses it under and the next team member tosses it over until it reaches the last player. He catches the ball and runs with it to the front of the line.

Repeat until the first person in each team has worked his way back to the front of the line. The first team to finish are the winners.

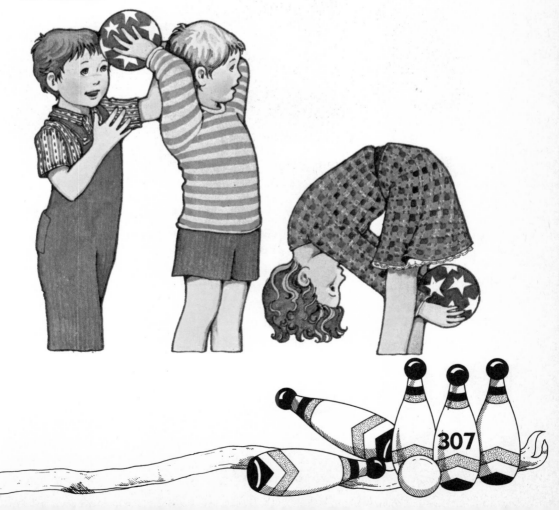

307

The odd man

Oscar was the oddest man you ever saw. His face was blue, his hair was pink, he wore trousers covered in small green tomatoes and he had feet the shape of long thin sausages. But, not only did he look odd, he *was* odd, too. His house was shaped like a flying saucer, and he slept in a hammock made of spaghetti under a banana-skin blanket. His chair was made out of cabbages and he had a pet dog that looked like a pink balloon on four legs, whose name was Lollipop.

One evening, Oscar sat in his cabbage chair, took a sip of acorn and butterscotch wine and said to Lollipop, 'You know, Lollipop, I'd love to be normal, just for a day.'

'Wuff,' agreed Lollipop.

And so, the very next day, Oscar woke up in a normal bed. He looked in the mirror and saw a normal man. Then he put on a normal shirt, tie, suit and shoes. Even Lollipop had become a normal-looking dog.

'I say, Lollipop, I do believe we're normal today,' said Oscar as he ate two slices of toast and marmalade for breakfast. Then he left his normal-looking house, with a rolled-up newspaper under his arm and Lollipop on a lead. They walked into town – how strange it was that no one stared at them as they normally did – and Oscar went and talked to the bank manager about normal old money matters. For lunch he ate a normal ham sandwich while Lollipop ate a normal bone. Then they went to the library where Oscar looked through a normal book on railways. Then they went to the post office to buy some normal stamps.

They returned home and, miraculously, before their very eyes, the normal house turned back into the flying saucer, Oscar's suit changed back into his odd clothes and his feet became two long thin sausages again. Meanwhile, Lollipop was again a pink balloon on four legs.

'Thank goodness for that,' said Oscar. 'I was beginning to worry that we'd never get back to normal – er, that is, get back to being odd.'

He sat down on his cabbage chair and took a large bite of fish finger covered in raspberry jam and chocolate sauce. 'I much prefer being odd,' he said opening a book called *The Toad Who Wore Pyjamas*. 'It's so boring being normal, don't you think, Lollipop?'

'Wuff,' agreed Lollipop, happily tucking into a large plateful of fruit trifle and chips.

The wine harvest

Roy and Rachel liked going into the greenhouse in their garden. Inside was a grapevine. It grew all along one side of the greenhouse and, in autumn, there were lots of bunches of green grapes on it.

One Sunday morning when their father was out, Rachel said, 'Let's make some wine, as a surprise!'

'How?' said Roy.

'With the grapes, of course,' said Rachel. 'It's easy – I saw it in a book. You just pick the grapes and then tread on them with your feet, and then put the juice into bottles.'

Roy thought it sounded odd, but he helped Rachel pick some bunches of grapes. They put them in a bucket, and Roy was just going to step into it to tread the grapes, when Rachel shouted, 'Wait! Take your shoes and socks off first!'

They took it in turns to stand in the bucket and stamp up and down on the grapes, which felt all squishy under their bare feet. They poured the juice through a strainer into a jug, and then into an empty lemonade bottle. Rachel made a label saying 'white wine' and stuck it on.

'Whatever's this?' said their father, as they all sat down to lunch.

'It's white wine. We made it!' cried Roy and Rachel together.

'How clever!' said their father. He poured out a small glass, held it up and sniffed it. 'It smells delicious,' he said, raising the glass to his lips.

'We trod it with our own feet!' said Roy proudly.

Their father stopped still, the glass in his hand. 'Really?' he said.

'That's how they do it in some countries, at the wine harvest,' Rachel said.

'I know,' said her father, 'and I've just remembered something else. They always keep the wine for a long time in the bottles, before they drink it. So I'd better pour this back, and we'll put the bottle in the cupboard. I'll look forward to drinking it . . . sometime.'

Roy and Rachel were a bit disappointed, but they cheered up when their father brought out a bottle of lemonade and poured some out for them. 'You'll like this,' he said. 'It's fresh from this year's lemonade harvest!'

Plan your home

You will need

Some paper
A pencil
A ruler
A rubber

Have you ever tried making a plan of a building? You imagine you're looking down on it from above and draw the shapes of the rooms, taking one floor at a time.

Try making a plan of your house. If you live in a flat or a bungalow it will be easier because you'll only have one level to draw. If you live in a house with three storeys it will take a little longer!

Remember to mark all the windows and doors and label every room. If you like you could make a really big plan and show all the main pieces of furniture in the rooms as well.

Once you've had some practice at drawing plans, why not draw a plan of your ideal home – the one where you'd most like to live?

312

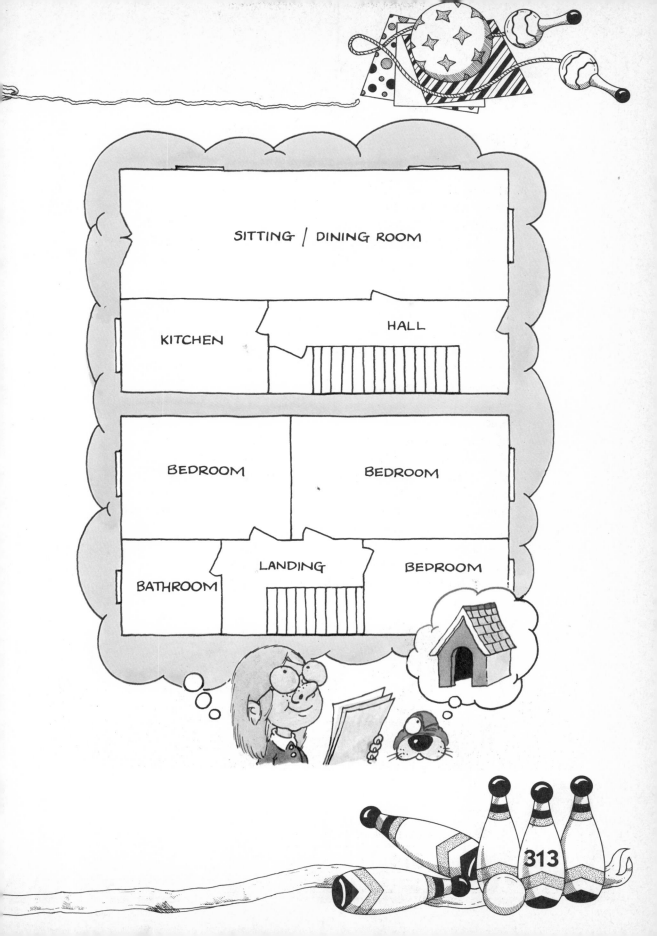

SITTING / DINING ROOM

KITCHEN

HALL

BEDROOM

BEDROOM

BATHROOM

LANDING

BEDROOM

313

The parcel

Sarah and Ben were playing in the garden one summer day, but they were hot and cross and kept quarrelling.

Ben snatched Sarah's doll out of its pram and pretended to throw it over the hedge. Sarah didn't like being teased and rode away on Ben's bike. Then their Uncle John came into the garden.

'Hello,' he said, 'I've brought you two a present as it's such a hot day.'

Ben and Sarah stopped looking cross and looked at Uncle John instead. He handed them a small, flat parcel.

'It's not very big,' he said, 'but give it air and water and it will grow into something lovely for you.'

The children were puzzled. 'The parcel is flat – it must be a book,' said Ben.

'I think it's a plant – they need air and water,' said Sarah. The children unwrapped the parcel, and there was a lovely brightly coloured paddling pool waiting to be unfolded and blown up.

Sarah gave Ben his bike back so that they could blow up the paddling pool with the pump, and then she ran to find the garden hose.

Uncle John helped the children to fill the pool with water and they had a great time splashing and paddling.

314

The king's statue

Long ago, in Persia (which is now called Iran), there lived a king so vain that he ordered a statue of himself to be built, which would be the biggest statue in the world.

'Put it up there, in the hills, where everyone can see it,' he said, 'and decorate it with the finest gold and jewels.'

His people were poor, and needed houses more than statues, but they had to obey. For years they toiled in the hot sun, hacking the stones out of the bare hills, and carving and cutting them.

When the statue was nearly finished, the king arranged a special ceremony. While his people lined the rocky ledges to watch, he himself started to dig out the final stone to finish the statue. But as he pulled the stone from the rock-face, a hidden underground river gushed out of the hole. The people watched as it swept the king away in its flood, never to be seen again.

The tumbling waters crashed against the statue, which began to crumble and sway. Suddenly, it toppled over, and crashed into the flood. The people scrambled and began to gather the gold and jewels washed up on the banks. Now they had finally been rewarded for all their hard work.

The red coat

One morning Susan and her mother were going to do the shopping. Susan's mother opened the wardrobe door and took out her coat.

'Why don't you wear this pretty red coat?' asked Susan pointing to it.

Mother laughed. 'Well, it's quite old,' she said, 'I'll have to give it to a jumble sale.'

'But it's such a nice colour,' argued Susan. 'Red's my favourite colour.'

Mother looked at the coat. 'Do you know, Susan,' she said, 'I've had an idea. I think I could use this material to make a dressing-gown for you. You need a new one.'

'Ooh, yes,' said Susan.

What a busy afternoon they had snipping and stitching and using the sewing-machine. Susan watched Mother making the little velvet collar and cuffs. Mother gave her

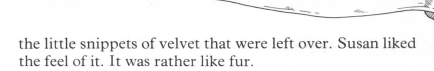

the little snippets of velvet that were left over. Susan liked
the feel of it. It was rather like fur.

At last Mother said, 'Nearly finished now – just the
buttons to put on.'

That night Susan *wanted* bedtime to come! She had her
bath early and then she put on her lovely new
dressing-gown. She counted the buttons, one, two, three,
four, five, six, seven, eight, nine, ten.

When she went downstairs Daddy said, 'Hello, little
robin redbreast. That's a lovely dressing-gown.' Then
Susan climbed on to his knee to hear her bedtime story.

Christmas tree

1

Make one cut into the centre of the circle of cardboard and then make a cone. Tape the edges together, then paint the cone green all over.

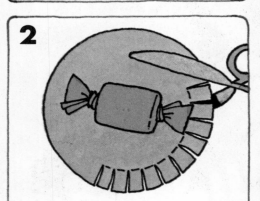

2

Cut out small circles of coloured paper and make little cuts around the edges of each circle to make a fringe. Stick small wrapped sweets in the centre of each circle of paper. Then stick the circles to the tree.

This is a nice decoration to put in the middle of your Christmas dinner table. Or you can hide little presents underneath it.

Father Christmas

YOU WILL NEED
A circle of thin cardboard
Cotton wool
Sticky tape
Non-toxic glue
Your paint box, felt pens or crayons
Scissors

1

Make one cut into the centre of the circle of cardboard and form a cone. Tape the edges together to hold the card in place.

3

Stick on cotton wool for hair and whiskers.

2

Draw on a face and paint the rest of the cone red.

Stars

Stars are a pretty decoration at any time of the year. Ask permission first and perhaps you will be allowed to stick a pattern of stars on your bedroom ceiling.

1

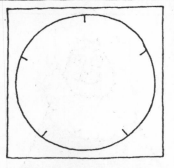

Draw a circle on the card using a saucer or small plate to draw round. Cut out the circle. Make five marks round the outside of the circle at roughly the same distance apart.

2

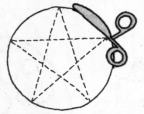

Join the marks using a ruler as shown. Cut out the star. If you want to make lots of stars use this first one as a pattern for the rest by drawing round it.

3

Decorate the stars using paints or pens, or cover them in silver or gold paper. If you want to hang the stars up, push a needle and cotton through one point and hang the star up by the thread.

Snowflakes

YOU WILL NEED
Sheet of plain paper
Scissors
Pencil
Saucer or plate

1

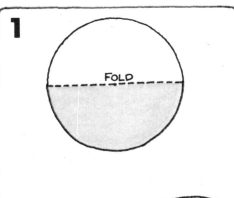

FOLD

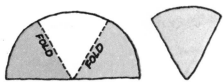

FOLD FOLD

Lay a saucer or small plate on the paper and draw round it. Cut out the circle of paper. Fold it in half and then into thirds.

2

Cut the pointed top off the cone shape and cut different shaped notches in the sides and bottom of the cone. Open out the paper and you have your snowflake.

3

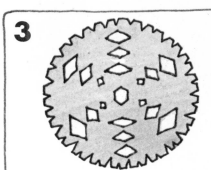

Snowflakes can be stuck on to windows for a Christmas decoration or use them as doilies on plates to make your party table look pretty.

Spinning spiral

YOU WILL NEED
Sheet of coloured paper or foil
A dinner plate
Pencil
Scissors
Needle and cotton

1

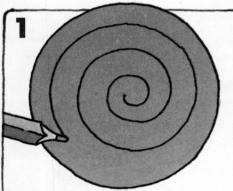

Put the plate on the coloured paper or foil and draw round it. Cut out the circle of paper and carefully draw a spiral on it beginning at the centre.

3

You can make a spinning spiral out of plain paper and colour it in if you like.

2

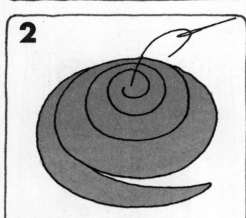

Cut along the line you have drawn. Sew a piece of cotton through the centre of the spiral to hang it up by.

322

Paper bell

YOU WILL NEED
Sheet of coloured paper
Scissors
Pencil
Saucer or plate
Ribbon

1

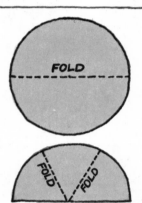

Put a saucer or small plate on the paper and draw round it. Cut out the circle of paper. Fold it in half and then into thirds.

2

Make cuts from side to side of the cone as shown. The closer the cuts are to each other the better.

3

Open the paper out very carefully and stretch the rings gently downwards. Hang the bell up using a piece of ribbon threaded through the top.

The water giant

Far away in the dark, thick forests of Germany lived two
angry giants who were always quarrelling. Their names were
Trog and Grog.

One day Trog was in his garden planting fir trees, which
he used for matchsticks, when he heard a deep growl behind
him. It was Grog.

'You've planted your trees on my land,' Grog said crossly.

'No I haven't,' answered Trog. 'This is my part of the
forest and I'll plant what I like here, so there!'

They started to push and heave at each other: Trog trying
to push Grog away from his trees and Grog trying to push
Trog off *his* land. They pushed and pushed but they were
both so strong that neither moved at all!

At last Grog got tired of pushing and, dropping to his
knees, began pulling at the ground beneath Trog's feet. 'If I

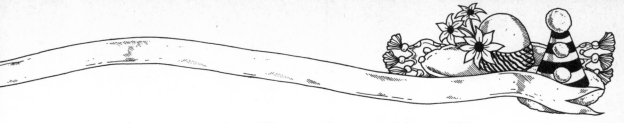

can't move you, then I'll move the ground instead,' he growled.

'Oh no you don't,' said Trog and he too began to tear at the ground.

They pulled and pulled until suddenly there was a terrible ripping sound and the land split open like an old cloth sack. The tear stretched as far as they could see. It went right across the land to the sea which flooded in filling up the hole completely.

'Now see what you've done, you stupid giants!' Trog and Grog jumped with surprise. Standing behind them was a strange figure dressed entirely in blue. He carried a great staff which was decorated from top to bottom with shells, fishes and beautiful water plants.

'Who are you?' they asked, a little frightened.

'I am the giant of the water places,' he answered in a strong voice. It seemed to flow right over the two sulky giants as they faced each other across the swift flowing river they had made.

'Now you must stay on your own banks. The water is mine and neither of you must ever cross the river again. If you do, I will turn you to stone with my magic.' With these words the water giant turned and slowly melted into the river.

Right up to this day the river Rhine still flows swiftly through the hills of Germany. If you travel there you will find two great rocks facing each other across the waters. So the silly giants must have tried to cross the river after all!

A blue handkerchief

Christopher was going to school. His Mummy said, 'Take this nice new handkerchief with you,' and she gave him a bright blue one.

Christopher ran to catch the school bus. As he ran, the handkerchief dropped out of his pocket, and lay on the ground.

Later, a man came walking along. 'What's this!' he exclaimed. He picked up the bright blue handkerchief.

'Just what I need for the sun, today!' he said, and he tied a knot in each corner. Then he put it on his head, and went off to work in the fields.

But a gust of wind blew the handkerchief off. Then, a lady with her shopping on a bicycle came along. She was trying hard to ride with a broken seat. She saw the blue handkerchief.

'Just what I need!' she cried. She tied the seat with it, and happily pedalled home.

At home, her little boy was crying. 'My kite won't fly!' he sobbed.

326

'Why,' she said, 'you've lost its tail.'

She took the handkerchief off her bicycle, and tied it to the kite. Up it soared, high into the air, the piece of bright blue flapping in the wind. But after a while, the wind tugged too much at the handkerchief, and tugged it off.

A little boy found it and used it to wrap up his collection of stones.

Later on, he bumped into Christopher. 'Look at my stones, Christopher!' he said, and took the blue handkerchief full of stones out of his pocket.

Christopher stared. 'That's my handkerchief!' he said.

'Is it really?' said the boy. 'Well you had better have it back, then!'

Later on, Christopher's Mummy saw the blue handkerchief.

'How on earth has it got into such a terrible state?' cried Mummy.

But Christopher couldn't answer, for how was *he* to know?

327

Self-portrait

You will need

Large piece of paper
Felt pen with thick tip

It is *very* difficult to draw a picture of yourself, but here's an easy way. It probably won't end up looking much like you but it's great fun to do!

Hold the piece of paper over your face with one hand and 'trace' your features with a felt tip pen on the other side of the paper.

Of course you won't be able to see what you're doing, you'll have to do it all by touch.

Speedy tortoises

You will need

Thin card
Your crayons or felt pens
Scissors
String

1 Take a piece of card and draw a large tortoise shape on it. Colour it in with crayons or felt pens. Make another tortoise about the same size and shape.

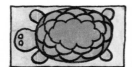

2 Cut out the tortoises and pierce a small hole at each end (front and back) quite near the edge.

3 Thread a long piece of string down through one hole and up through the other. Do this with both tortoises.

4 Tie one end of the string to a table leg about as high up the leg as the tortoise is long. Tie the end of the other string to the other table leg. Your race is now ready to begin.

5 Race the tortoises by sitting on the floor well away from the table. Start off with the tortoise at your end of the string, hold the string taut and twitch it so that the tortoise 'races' along the string. (You may need to practise this a little first.) The first tortoise to get to the table is the winner.

329

Skating

Cathy jumped out of bed, and pulled back the curtains. The window was so frozen, she couldn't see out at all.

She pressed her warm fingers on the pane and made peepholes.

Everything was white with thick frost. The shallow river running by their home was still and hard.

She ran downstairs. 'Look at the weather!' she cried. 'The river is frozen!'

'I know,' said Mummy. 'Daddy is outside with Stephen, testing it.'

Stephen was Cathy's elder brother. He came dashing in, cheeks glowing, eyes bright.

'It's solid, Mummy!' he said excitedly. 'Where are my skates?'

'*I* want to skate,' said Cathy.

Daddy came in, stamping his feet. 'It's safe enough,' he said. 'In fact, some neighbours are skating already.'

'*I* want to skate!' cried Cathy, again.

'You're too little,' said Stephen.

'No I'm not!' Cathy was cross. 'Not this year!'

'Well you haven't any skates!' said Stephen, finding his. But when he tried them on – they wouldn't fit him anymore!

'Never mind,' said Daddy. 'I'll try to get you some, later.'

'I'll have to slide with my wellingtons,' said Stephen.

But the skates fitted Cathy – with two pairs of socks, that is. She could hardly wait to start skating.

They both went outside. Cathy gasped. The air was so keen, and the world around so beautiful. It was like a white wonderland.

People were skating quickly along, dressed in warm, bright clothes, with scarves flying.

Stephen joined them, sliding about. 'Wait for me!' cried Cathy. She copied the others, pushing her feet across the ice. And fell.

She tried again. And sat down with a thump. Stephen thought it a huge joke. No matter how Cathy tried, she could *not* skate.

After a while, Stephen, still laughing, ran off.

Cathy tried again, then stayed down, disheartened.

Suddenly, a bicycle came along – someone was riding a bicycle on the river! It was Stephen.

'Stand up,' he said, 'and hold on to the bike. I'll *pull* you along!'

So Cathy skated after all. She hung on tight, and they whizzed past the other skaters.

They had a lovely time. 'We're the fastest pair on ice!' they laughed.

Broken bottles

You will need:
a ball

This is a good warming-up game for rounders because it gives you practice in catching and throwing the ball.

Find a few friends – six would be about the right number. They should stand in a circle with one player in the middle. He throws the ball to each of the others in turn. They must try and catch it. If a player drops the ball he must pay for his mistake the next time round – he must catch the ball with one hand only. If he drops it again, he must catch it with the other hand when it is next thrown to him. The next penalty is to catch it while he is on one knee, then two knees and finally sitting down. If the player does not catch it sitting down, he is out. If the player catches it again before he is out, he can go back through all the positions in the next rounds until he is standing again.

Manhunt

You will need four players for this hide and seek game and you can have more if you want to.

Choose one person to hide. She runs off while the rest of the players count to a hundred with their eyes shut. They must not peep.

The person who is hiding can move about as much as she wants to, as long as she remains hidden. The others search for her. As soon as someone spots her, everybody gives chase. The first person to catch her is the next one to run and hide.

The snowman

Pamela and Seán loved the snow, so when they woke up one morning and saw the garden crisp and sparkling white, they ran downstairs laughing excitedly.

'Mummy, can we go out and play?' Seán asked, tugging at his mother's apron.

'Oh, yes, can we?' Pamela joined in eagerly.

Their mother laughed. 'Of course you can,' she said. 'As soon as you've had breakfast.'

When they'd eaten every bit of their hot porridge, they ran upstairs to dress in their warmest clothes and wellingtons.

'Come on, Pamela,' Seán urged his sister. 'We'll build the biggest snowman ever.'

They worked really hard gathering the snow into a huge pile for the snowman's body. Seán made it into a round, fat shape, while Pamela collected more snow for his head. By lunchtime, the snowman was as big as Seán.

'Mummy, have you got an old hat and a scarf for him?' Pamela asked. 'He needs them to keep him warm.'

'Oh, I think I can find something,' their mother said. 'What are you going to use for his eyes?'

'I've found two round stones,' Seán said, 'and a piece of stick for his mouth.'

By teatime, the snowman was finished. His hat was one of Seán's woolly caps, and he wore Daddy's oldest scarf. The stick Seán used for his mouth, made the snowman look as though he was smiling. Seán and Pamela thought he was magnificent.

When Daddy came home, they were longing to show him what they'd been doing.

'He's marvellous,' Daddy laughed. 'And my old scarf

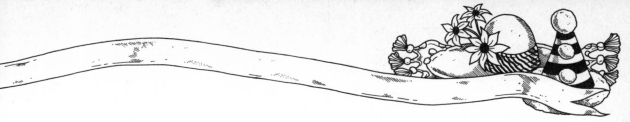

looks very good around his neck.'

By then it was getting quite dark and it was time for the children to go to bed. Seán stood by the window for a long time looking at their snowman. He looked so lonely out there all by himself. It was very cold in the garden and it was beginning to snow again. It seemed cruel to leave him there while Seán and Pamela were snuggling up cosy and warm in their beds.

'Mummy, can we bring our snowman in by the fire?' Seán asked. 'I don't want him to have to stay in the garden all night on his own.'

Seán's mother laughed. 'I think he'd prefer to stay outside, Seán,' she said. 'Snowmen don't like fires.'

Mr Horrible

Everything about Mr Horrible was horrible. He looked horrible, he smelt horrible, he was horrible to children. He lived in a horrible house and had a horrible rat for a pet. Mr Horrible actually enjoyed being horrible because then no one in the village would come and pester him.

Mr Horrible's neighbours, who lived in a big grand house next door, couldn't stand him being so horrible. He'd do horrible things like throw his horrible potato peelings over their roses and let his horrible rat chase their dog. He played horrible music very late at night, and when they politely said

'good morning' to him, Mr Horrible would always say, 'What's good about it? I think it's a *horrible* morning.'

One day the neighbours decided they had had enough of Mr Horrible, and so they moved to a house at the other end of the village. The estate agent had great trouble selling the house, partly because it was so big and partly because no one wanted to live next to Mr Horrible.

Now Lord and Lady Snooty-Snodgrass, who were very, very snobbish, and very rude, were looking for a house in the country, and so they went to look at the house next to Mr Horrible.

'What an odd little village,' said Lady Snooty-Snodgrass as they drove through it in their huge shiny car. 'I hope there is a dry-cleaner who will not ruin my mink coat when I have it cleaned.'

'I hope I can find a shop that sells sensible things such as champagne and oysters,' said Lord Snooty-Snodgrass. The people in the village looked on with loathing. Why, these people were worse than Mr Horrible! They hoped they wouldn't like the house.

But they loved it! It was big enough to give balls for their rich snobbish friends *and* house all their servants. But just as they had decided to buy it, they spied Mr Horrible with his horrible rat over the garden fence. When he saw them he gave them his most horrible look.

'I will not live next to such a horrible man,' declared Lady Snooty-Snodgrass loudly. 'Why, he'll give me nightmares.'

And so that was that. Thanks to Mr Horrible, they didn't buy the house. Everyone in the village was delighted.

The house never did get sold, and eventually the council decided to turn it into a museum. Everyone was very pleased, especially Mr Horrible, because it meant that his neighbours would be old farming tools, and they were hardly likely to pester him!

Wheelbarrow race

This is a race for people to do in pairs. You will need a grassy area to play it on.

One person walks on his hands while his partner holds his legs up in the air. The aim of each 'wheelbarrow' pair is to get to the finish line as fast as possible.

They can swap places and have another race.

338

Charades

This is a game for the whole family. It is a good one to play at a weekend, especially if you are staying inside.

The rules are very simple. Divide the players into two teams. One team goes out of the room to prepare their charade. They choose a word of two or three syllables such as 'cotton' or 'carpet'. They work out how they will act out the syllables and finally the whole word (*car,* then *pet,* then *carpet,* for example).

When they go back into the room they act the charade. Before they start acting, the leader of the team should show how many syllables the word has by holding up the right number of fingers. He should also show whether it is the first, second or third syllable which is going to be acted. If a syllable is very difficult to act, the team can act a different word which sounds like it, for example by acting *wet* instead of *pet.* The leader first holds his hand up to his ear to show that the word 'sounds like'.

The other team has to try and guess what the word is. When they have guessed, they have a turn.

The moorhens

The sun was just rising above the farmer's fields. The cock in the chicken shed began to crow. In the big pond at the bottom of the farm a moorhen swam quietly out from among the tall reeds. Her black and white tail flicked back and forth. Her red eyes looked around. There was no-one about. She gave a croak and two baby moorhens swam out of the reeds. They were black and fluffy.

The mother dived under the water. The chicks tried to follow. They ducked their heads and paddled. But they were too light to go under. They just swam along with their tails in the air.

The mother rose to the surface a few yards ahead. The family climbed on to the shore and began to nibble the weeds and grass there.

Slowly they grazed farther and farther from the pond. Now they were on the edge of the farmer's lawn. On one side was his house, on the other his vegetable garden. Cautiously, watching the house the mother led her family across the open lawn.

When they reached the garden the mother went first to the lettuce. She tore off the outer leaves and ate them. The chicks ate the soft centres.

340

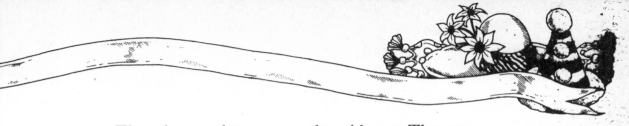

Then the moorhen went to the cabbages. They were tightly-packed but the mother jabbed her beak through the hard outer leaves. The chicks stuck their bills into the holes and ate and ate.

Suddenly there was a startled cry from above. 'Out of my garden, you pests!' the farmer shouted. He had come out to weed his garden. Swinging his hoe he came at the moorhens.

The little family scattered. They ran across the lawn, their necks outstretched, their bodies bent forward. The farmer ran right behind them waving his hoe.

When the birds reached the pond the mother dived under the water. And this time, paddling furiously, the chicks did too.

When the chicks came out of the water they were in the centre of the reeds. Their mother was already in the nest. They crawled in under her.

Night fell. Now it was the end of the day. In the trees around the pond an owl hooted. In the distance a fox barked.

And in the farmhouse the farmer made plans to fence in his garden the next day.

The steel band

Winston's big brother was loading his steel drum into a small trailer on the back of his bicycle.

'Can I come and play in the steel band?' asked Winston.

'Perhaps when you're older,' said Joe.

Winston kicked at a stone and wandered off to the river. He sat on the bank trailing a stick in the water. After a few minutes an oil drum came floating downstream. Winston waded a little way into the water. It was quite shallow and with his stick he managed to stop the oil drum and guide it to the bank.

He found a couple of sticks and began to beat the oil drum. It made a good, hollow sound, but nothing like a proper West Indian steel drum.

'What's that racket you're making, Winston?' asked Mr Montgomery who was passing by.

'I'm playing my steel drum,' said Winston.

'I see,' said Mr Montgomery laughing. 'Come to my workshop and we'll see if we can make a real steel drum for you.'

Mr Montgomery cut the oil drum in half. Then he hammered the end into shape, so that he could play different notes on different parts of the drum.

'There's an old pair of drumsticks on the shelf, Winston. You try.'

342

Winston thanked Mr Montgomery and went off to practise. Every day he went down to the river and practised hard until he could play lots of tunes.

The day of the holiday parade arrived and Joe had to go on his bicycle to the other end of the island. 'I'll be back for the parade at noon,' he promised.

At noon, however, there was no sign of Joe, and the parade was ready to start.

'What shall we do?' said the leader of the steel band.

Winston spoke up. 'I can play instead,' he said. 'I've been practising.'

He ran home to fetch his steel drum. He played a few notes rapidly round the drum.

'That's good,' said the leader. 'Join the band.'

Winston felt very proud as he marched along the road playing with the band. As the parade reached the town square, Joe rode up. 'I'm sorry I missed the parade,' he said. 'My bike had a puncture on the other side of the island and I couldn't get back in time.'

'Well, thanks to Winston, everything was fine,' said the leader of the band. 'Next time you must both play.'

Stairs marathon

You will need

A flight of stairs
An old but heavy book

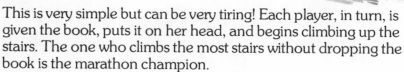

This is very simple but can be very tiring! Each player, in turn, is given the book, puts it on her head, and begins climbing up the stairs. The one who climbs the most stairs without dropping the book is the marathon champion.

One minute walk

You will need

A watch with a second hand

One person is the 'starter' and has the watch. Everyone else takes off their watches. (Cover up any clocks in the room too.)

The starter lines everyone up on one side of the room and tells them they have exactly sixty seconds to cross it. The players then have to judge for themselves how slowly they must walk to reach the other side of the room in exactly one minute. Walking backwards and sideways are not allowed!

345

Cold spells

One day the wizard found none of his spells would work. He had a spell to make the kettle boil which he used in the morning to make his cup of tea, but that wouldn't work. He had a spell which made toast for his breakfast, but that wouldn't work either.

'Whatever is the matter!' he said crossly. 'It's very cold today and I need a nice hot cup of tea and a lovely piece of

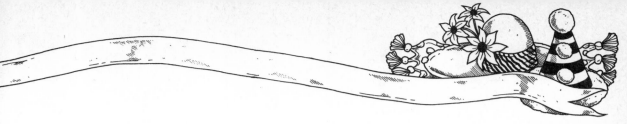

hot, buttered toast. I can't understand it.'

In the end he had to go and ask the advice of the witch who lived next door.

'That is strange,' she said, when the wizard had explained what was the matter. 'I'll look in my spell book and see if I can find a spell to cure spells that won't work.'

She walked over to the shelf to fetch her spell book. Her big black cat was sitting right on top of it. 'That's right, Puss,' she said. 'You sit up there and keep my spells warm.'

The big black cat stretched and yawned and purred.

'How do you keep your spells warm in this cold weather?' the witch asked the wizard.

'How do I keep my spells warm!' said the wizard in amazement. 'Why should I do that?'

'Don't you know that spells have to be kept warm?' said the witch in surprise. 'The cat keeps my spells warm. He sleeps on top of my spell book. If spells get cold they won't work at all.'

'Oh dear,' said the wizard. 'That's what is wrong with my spells then. I didn't know they had to be kept warm. I haven't been a wizard very long. I only passed my wizard exams in the summer.'

'Goodness me,' said the witch. 'I don't know what they teach you at wizard school these days. Fancy not knowing that you must keep your spells warm.'

'What can I do?' asked the wizard. 'Wizards don't have cats.'

'I tell you what,' said the witch. 'I'll lend you my everlasting hot water bottle to put on top of your spell book until you can get down to the magic shop and buy one for yourself.'

So the wizard's spells worked again, and the first spell he did was to magic up a big bunch of roses to give to the witch next door.

Peter's penny

The question is: why did Peter Pingle pass the sweet shop that afternoon without a pause?

That day, that very morning, Peter Pingle had but one penny. What could he, the sweet shop's best customer, buy with just one penny? He tossed the coin in the air. The penny missed his outstretched hand, fell on the pavement and rolled swiftly away.

After it, Peter ran, but as fast as he ran the coin rolled faster. Down the street, through the town, into the country they both raced.

Suddenly the penny stopped. Peter stopped too and looked around. He had never seen this place before. Toffees and aniseed balls covered a golden beach. Frothy waves from a pink milk-shake sea beat on the shore.

Peter turned about. A jungle lay behind. Giant trees of lollipops were hung with peppermint sticks. Chocolate berries swung from licorice vines. Beside a lemon-squash pool grew caramel bushes.

'No need to spend me then,' the penny said at Peter's feet. 'Instead enjoy yourself here for a day.'

And that is why Peter Pingle, on his way back home, passed that sweet shop without a pause.

348

Mad March Hare

Mad March Hare woke up one morning and quivered his whiskers. 'Spring is on the way,' he thought. 'Soon the sun will grow warmer and the days longer, and I must find a nice field to live in,' and away he ran in search of a field. Soon he came to a fine green place where the sun shone all day.

'This will do for me,' thought March Hare, and he was so pleased with his new field that he skipped around in circles and jumped high in the air like an acrobat.

'What do you think you're doing in my field?' asked a cross voice suddenly.

March Hare twirled round – and there was another hare!

'*Your* field?' asked March Hare. 'Nonsense! This is *my* field!'

'Oh no, it isn't.'

'Oh yes, it is.'

This argument went on for quite some time, and the two hares became so bad-tempered that they started to fight. But the fight didn't last long. March Hare won, and he chased the other hare off to find himself a field somewhere else.

Then he began to skip and jump and somersault around his field all over again. He looked so funny! If you'd have seen him, you'd have said he really was a Mad March Hare!

Printing

You can print with almost anything – the end of a cotton reel, vegetables, leaves, kitchen implements – even your hands and feet. Printing is just a method of putting paint or ink on one surface and pressing that surface on to paper. Printing is useful because it means you can make the same shape over and over again which is useful for making patterns and borders.

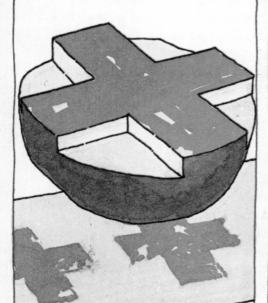

A potato is good to print with because you can cut a raised pattern in the potato. Cut the potato in half. Then dig out a simple design on the flat ends, brush on paint and then press the potato on to your paper. A potato print on tissue paper in thick paint makes unusual wrapping paper.

YOU WILL NEED
2 or 3 potatoes
Potato peeler
Collection of different shaped leaves
Sheets of plain and tissue paper
Non-toxic paints

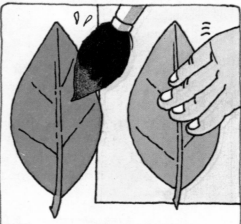

To make a leaf print, collect as many different leaves as you can. Take each leaf in turn and paint all over one side of it. Don't use too much paint. Press the painted side of the leaf down on to your paper.

Don't forget to try experimenting with other ways of printing.

Mosaic

On the card lightly sketch in with a pencil an outline for your picture. Instead of colouring the picture in – cut out small squares of coloured paper from old magazines and stick them on until the picture is filled in.

YOU WILL NEED
Piece of thick paper or card
Old magazines
Scissors
Non-toxic glue
Pencil

Clever Ki-ki

In the green rain-forests of South America, the vast Amazon river gleams through the steamy jungle.

Mayta, a native girl, lived in a thatched village by the river. She was well-known by all the tribe, for she had a blue and yellow macaw, named Ki-ki. Mayta had found the macaw while walking in the forest. Ki-ki was a baby bird and lost, so Mayta looked after him, and now the bird would not leave her side.

'I shall teach him to talk!' Mayta told her friends.

'Talk!' scoffed one boy, called Capac. 'I would rather have it cooked for dinner!'

Mayta walked away crossly and gave Ki-ki some nuts, his favourite food. 'Here's a nut,' Mayta would say, and Ki-ki could crack open even the hardest nut with his beak.

So it wasn't surprising that when Ki-ki started to speak, the only thing he would say, was 'Here's a nut!'

But Capac didn't laugh. He was jealous of the way Ki-ki followed Mayta everywhere. 'Stupid thing!' he scowled, and determined to catch the macaw.

But one day, when all the children had been playing in the jungle, Capac did not come back with them.

'Where can he be?' asked Mayta, worried. 'Soon it will be dusk.' No one should be alone in the jungle at dusk. For then, the wild-cats and jaguars prowl. They waited, but Capac did not come.

'We must go back and look for him,' said Mayta. So they set off, into the jade-green twilight.

'Go find Capac!' Mayta ordered Ki-ki. The macaw squawked and flew on ahead.

'Capac!' the children shouted, but there was no answer. Suddenly Ki-ki started to screech loudly and they ran towards the noise.

'Capac!' called Mayta.

'Here!' came back a voice, mixed with Ki-ki's screeches.

They found him, lying on the ground with a sprained ankle.

'I'm glad to see you,' he gasped, thankfully. 'It will soon be dark.'

'We must hurry,' said Mayta. 'Thank goodness Ki-ki found you so quickly,' and the others agreed.

Capac hung his head. 'I'm sorry I was nasty about him,' he said. 'From now on, I promise I'll be his friend.'

Mayta was pleased. So was Ki-ki. He squawked and flew around, then landed on Capac's head.

'Here's a nut!' he screeched, 'Here's a nut!'

And everyone laughed.

School freeze

This was the coldest winter for sixty years according to the weathermen. Ben and Alice could believe them. They looked out of their window on Monday morning to see the ground covered with a hard white frost. Their father's car looked white too although really it was bright yellow.

'I'll never get it started,' he said. 'I feel like staying in bed today and not going to work.'

'Oh, so do we,' said Ben and Alice. 'Let's not go to school. It's such a long way.'

'What nonsense,' said Mother. 'It's a few minutes walk, and school is lovely and warm, and your father *is* going to work.'

Dad made a face and winked at Ben and Alice, who laughed.

Mother walked the children to school to show that the cold was really nothing much, then hurried back home again. Ben and Alice settled in their classroom. It really was quite warm there.

As morning wore on though, the classroom began to get very cold and the children shivered.

'You're imagining it children,' said Miss Griffiths, their teacher, when they complained, but she too was getting very cold.

354

Suddenly Amy Holland screamed. 'Look,' she cried, 'there's water pouring under the door.'

There certainly was. Miss Griffiths led all the children out to the hall. All the other classes were coming in there too. The headmistress sent for Thomas the caretaker.

'What *has* happened?' she asked him.

'All the pipes have burst, I'm afraid,' he said.

'Well, the school will have to be closed for a few days,' said the headmistress, 'until the pipes are mended.' All the children cheered and yelled.

'Let's go and skate on the pond,' said Ben to Alice.

'I'm going to roast chestnuts,' said Amy Holland.

Even Miss Griffiths was secretly pleased. She thought that she would prepare some lessons at home while toasting her feet by the fire, and drinking lots of hot tea.

Only Pipkin the school cat was annoyed. He usually slept in the boiler room and now he would have to find somewhere else for a few nights.

Magic handkerchief

You will need

A large handkerchief

This trick needs a bit of practice before you can show it to anyone, but once you've got the knack, it looks very impressive.

When you do the trick in front of an audience you produce a large handkerchief and say, 'This is a magic handkerchief, it can tie knots in itself!' Wave it about so that everyone can see it, then flip it from the corner, hard, several times until suddenly a knot appears in one corner – by magic!

In fact, you tie the knot in the corner before the audience arrives, but when you wave the handkerchief in front of them you keep your hand over the knot. The last time that you flip the handkerchief you drop the knotted corner and catch it by another corner, so quickly that no one notices you do it.

A very silly trick

You will need

A sheet of paper
Your crayons or felt pens
Scissors

This trick really is very silly but most people like it!

Take a piece of paper and draw a large, funny face on it, but instead of drawing a nose, draw a small circle. Carefully cut out the circle to make a round hole in the middle of the paper.

Turn the paper over and write in large letters around the hole: PUT YOUR THUMB IN HERE AND TURN THE PAPER OVER TO SEE A PICTURE OF YOURSELF.

Now give the paper to an unsuspecting friend, writing side up.

The castle ghost

There was a ruined castle near the village where Donald and
Jean lived, and a ghost was said to roam among the stone
walls, moaning and groaning.

One cold, dark evening, Donald and Jean dared each
other to go to the castle! They pretended to be very brave
as they climbed the gate into the field where the ruins stood.
The walls loomed up black and unfriendly against the sky,
and the wind seemed to whisper in the dark corners.

'Perhaps there isn't any ghost,' said Jean.

'Even if there is,' said Donald, 'I'm not scared of it!'

'Nor am I!' said Jean.

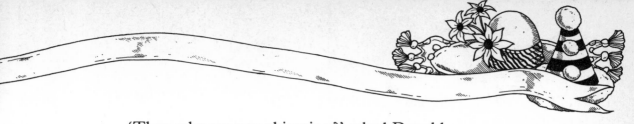

'Then why are you shivering?' asked Donald.

'I'm cold, that's all,' Jean said. 'Besides, you're shivering too.'

'No, I'm not,' said Donald.

'Yes, you are,' Jean persisted.

'No, I'm not,' said Donald.

'Shush!' whispered Jean suddenly. 'Listen! I thought I heard footsteps.'

They clutched each other and listened. Sure enough, someone, or something, was treading heavily on the grass, just behind the wall where they stood.

'It's the ghost!' whispered Donald. 'What shall we do?'

'Stay quite still,' said Jean. 'It may go away again without seeing us.'

Just then, from behind the wall, came a terrifying sound, like a loud, deep moan.

Donald and Jean gasped, and started to run, through the ruins and across the field. They scrambled over the gate and ran and ran, until they fell in at the door of their parents' cottage.

'Whatever have you two been doing?' asked their mother.

'We were just having a race,' gasped Donald.

'Well, get yourselves washed, and I'll give you some tea,' said their mother.

When they were ready for tea, their father came in and said he'd just met Farmer Moffatt, bringing back one of his cows that had strayed into the castle.

'Mr Moffatt said it was mooing away as if it was really upset,' said their father. 'He wondered if it had seen the ghost!'

He laughed. Donald and Jean looked at each other. So *that* was what they had heard – Farmer Moffatt's cow, tramping about, and then starting to moo. They began to join in the laughter. . . .

Early closing day

Carol's dad was looking after her while her mum went shopping. Carol wasn't happy about it. She was very cross. She wanted to go to the shops with her mum.

So, she decided to do something very naughty indeed. She decided to follow her mum to the shops. She would take Emma, her rag doll, and her dolls' pram.

Her dad was busy in the kitchen. Carol could get to the shops and back before he finished.

She tucked Emma carefully into her pram and fetched her shopping basket. She felt proud of Emma as she pushed her along. The rag doll looked very pretty in her blue flowered bonnet and matching dress.

Carol stopped and pointed. 'Look, Emma. Look at those big, red flowers in Mrs Benson's garden.'

Carol chatted to Emma as they walked down the street. She forgot she was being naughty. She forgot that her dad would be very cross and worried if he found that she had gone.

She even forgot about the busy, main road that they had to cross. Today she was lucky. The road was not as busy as usual. She looked right, left and right again. There were no cars. Quickly, she pushed Emma across.

360

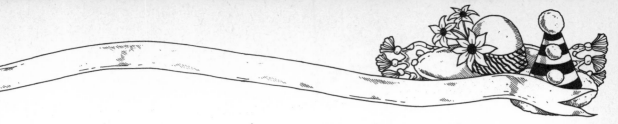

Soon, they were at the shops. First, she went to the butcher's and parked the pram outside the window. 'Now be a good girl, Emma,' she said. 'I won't be long.'

But the door of the butcher's shop was locked. She couldn't open it. The big supermarket was closed as well. She wheeled Emma to the other shops but it was the same everywhere.

It was very strange. All the shops were shut and there was no one walking about. How would she find her mum?

Then she heard someone running. She turned round. It was her dad. She ran to him and he hugged and hugged her. When he stopped hugging her, he became very cross. He told her what a bad girl she had been. 'You could have been killed on that busy road,' he said. He explained that the shops closed early that day. Her mum had gone right into the town on the bus. Carol would never have found her.

When they got home, her dad made them both a cup of tea. Carol felt safe and happy. She would never, ever go shopping by herself again.

Balloon relay race

You will need:
some balloons

Have lots of people for this game and play it outside. Divide everyone into teams and give each team a balloon.

The first person in each team puts the balloon between her knees and runs to the other end of the track and back. Using her knees, she then passes the balloon to the next person in the team. She must not drop the balloon. If she does, she must go back to the start.

The relay continues until all team members have run once. The first team to finish are the winners.

362

Harold and Gertrude

You will need:
an old newspaper
a blindfold (a scarf or piece of cloth)

Choose two people to be Harold and Gertrude. Blindfold Harold, give him a rolled-up newspaper, and put him in the middle of the circle of children. He calls out 'Gertrude'. Gertrude must answer 'Harold'. Harold tries to find her by the sound of her voice. He has to try and hit her with the newspaper. She runs round the outside of the circle.

When he succeeds he can take off the blindfold. Gertrude then wears the blindfold and tries to find Harold with the newspaper.

While this is going on, the other children will be in the way. They must keep out of the way of the newspaper, without letting go of each others' hands. Anyone who is hit by the newspaper is out.

The beaver

Long ago in the great forests of Canada the animals held a meeting.

The moose said, 'It is good living in this forest. Our homes are safe.'

The muskrat agreed. 'We have plenty to eat.'

'If only we had water in the hot summer,' said the wolf. 'But then the river runs away into the valley, and there is too little to drink.'

'Perhaps we could catch the river in winter, and keep it somehow,' said the moose.

The animals scratched their heads.

'I think I know what to do,' said the beaver who had been silent until then. He smiled and his big strong teeth flashed in the sunlight.

The beaver began to gnaw round the bottom of a tall tree standing on the riverbank. He gnawed until the tree began to sway from side to side then crash! It fell across the river.

The beaver gnawed at another tree until it too fell across the river with a great crash.

The beaver gnawed and gnawed until the river could no longer run away into the valley. It was trapped behind a wall of trees.

And the next summer the animals had all the water they needed, thanks to the beaver.

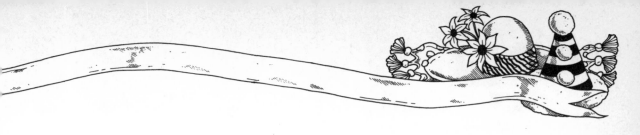

The clean pig

Dapper was a very fussy pig. Although he lived in a sty with all the other pigs he didn't care for their dirty habits – snorting, pushing and rooting around in the muck.

'I was pink as a piglet!' he shouted over the sty wall, 'and now look at me – I'm a sort of nasty patchy colour.'

He shouted again, 'Why must I live in this awful smelly place? I want to be clean. I want a bath.'

'Feel free to use my trough,' Thomas the horse suggested.

'How kind,' smiled Dapper, 'I'll have a bath straightaway.'

Dapper had a lovely bath in the horse trough and came out all pink. He rolled in the grass to dry off. Then back he trotted to the sty.

'Phew, Dapper's so dirty he's turning green and mouldy,' said the pigs.

'*I've* just had a bath!' Dapper insisted.

'Well, you are all green!' said the other pigs.

When Dapper had rolled in the grass, it had stained him green all over.

How the other pigs laughed. Now Dapper doesn't go on about being clean so much any more!

The snow picnic

Colin and Kate looked out of the kitchen window. It was a lovely crisp October morning. The hills were ablaze with autumn colour. Trees sparkled copper gold in the sunshine and the leaves made a lovely crunching sound as the wind blew them about.

'Can we go out, Mummy?' asked Colin.

'Yes dear. But wrap up warmly. It's quite chilly this morning.'

'May we take something to eat?' said Kate, looking at a pile of freshly baked cakes.

'What a good idea,' said Colin. 'We can have a picnic!'

'A picnic in October?' laughed Mummy. But she gathered together some of the cakes, and put them in a bag with two apples, some chocolate and a bottle of lemonade.

Colin and Kate set out across the field. They stopped to say hello to the farmer's cows, then jumped over the stile at the bottom of the field, and climbed up the steep hill.

Their favourite place was right at the top of the hill. It was a large oak tree with a hollow trunk. They climbed

366

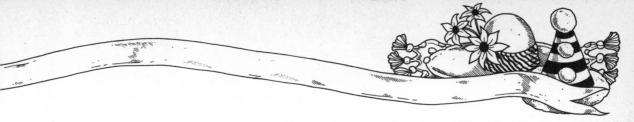

inside and munched happily on the chocolate bars. Kate had brought a card game, so they played two games of 'snap'.

Kate pulled her woolly hat further over her ears. 'Gosh, it's turning cold,' she shivered.

'Let's play outside,' said Colin. 'We will soon get warm.'

They jumped out of the tree. But instead of falling on a bed of leaves, they found the ground blanketed with cold white snow.

'Snow?' said Kate. 'Snow!' shouted Colin. 'What a surprise!' He gathered a handful and threw it at Kate. She laughed and threw one back. They had a wonderful time in the snow, running and jumping and rolling about. They made a snowman and a snow house, and then decided to have their picnic.

'A snow picnic!' laughed Kate.

'Yum,' said Colin, his mouth full of cake. They sat on the big curling roots of the oak tree and ate the cakes and apples. Snowflakes fell gently all around them. Kate tried to count them, but there were far too many. They finished off the chocolate and washed it down with lemonade.

'That was the best picnic I have ever had,' said Kate, and Colin agreed.

Papier mâché models

To model with papier mâché you need to make a softer mixture than for covering moulds and it takes longer to prepare.

WALLPAPER PASTE

1

Tear about 40 sheets of newspaper into very small pieces and put all the pieces in a bucket. Cover the paper with water and let it stand for 24 hours. Then pour off and squeeze out the surplus water. Add a cupful of wallpaper paste made up according to the instruction on the packet.

2

Knead the mixture until it feels like soft clay.

Now you can make all kinds of models. Leave them to dry in a warm place and after a few days you can paint them. If you want to make a large model, use a box as a base. You can varnish the models too if you like.

Yoghurt pot people

YOU WILL NEED
Yoghurt pots
Sheets of plain paper
Scraps of card and wool
Sticky tape
Non-toxic glue
Your paint box, felt pens or crayons
Scissors

1

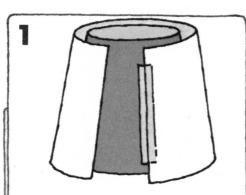

Turn the clean yoghurt pots upside down and cover them with paper. Fasten the paper around them with sticky tape.

2

Paint on faces, add wool for hair and cut out thin card shapes for arms, shoes and hats.

Daydreaming

Joey wandered slowly across the park on his way home from his friend's house. He was pretending to be a footballer. Suddenly, he heard loud barking and stopped his daydreaming. A huge dog was bounding towards him from the other side of the park. Joey was rather afraid of big dogs, so he decided that it would be a good idea to hide before the dog spotted him.

Joey crawled into a hole at the bottom of a nearby tree. It was dark and smelt like the cellar in his house which was very old. He waited and heard the barking dog run past. Then a man's voice shouted and the dog ran back again. It was safe to crawl out of the tree.

When he stood in the park again, Joey was surprised. The sun was shining brightly now, but when he had crawled into the tree, the sky had been cloudy. He was even more surprised when he came out of the park and walked along the road towards his home. Instead of cars there were carriages pulled by horses. All the people in the carriages

370

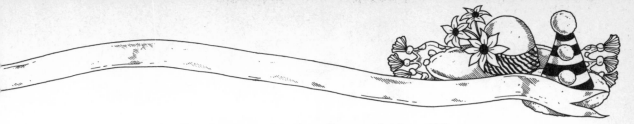

and in the street were wearing funny clothes. The women had dresses down to their ankles, and the men had long jackets and trousers which only came to their knees. It was like a picture he had seen in a book at school, showing how people had looked two hundred years ago. Perhaps it was some sort of carnival.

Joey arrived at his house and knocked on the door. Instead of his mum at the door, a tall woman with a long dress and apron, and a white, frilly cap on her head, stood there. She shouted at Joey, 'Clear off! I'm tired of you lot coming begging!' She slammed the door.

Joey didn't know what to do. Just then, a group of children came round the corner. *They* were wearing strange clothes too. They saw Joey and whispered to each other. Then they started laughing at him. They seemed to think *he* looked odd.

Joey ran away back to the park and the safety of the hole in the tree. Once more, when all was peaceful outside, he crawled out. The sky had clouded over again. He ran back home and knocked on the door. His mum opened the door and said, 'Where have you been? Your tea's ready.'

Joey just smiled. Everything was back to normal. He'd probably fallen asleep inside that tree. Or had he?

Debbie's diary

Debbie was very bored. She had been ill for over a week and she was tired of being in bed. 'I have nothing to do,' she grumbled.

'I have an idea,' said her mother. 'I'll move your bed over near the window and you can look out and watch everything that's going on.'

When her bed had been moved, Debbie could see the garden gate and right down to the post box at the corner.

'Now,' said her mother, 'why don't you keep a diary and write down what happens during the day?'

'All right,' said Debbie. Secretly she thought the diary would be very dull, but her brother, Hugh, gave her one of his old exercise books, so she started the diary straightaway.

That evening, she read the diary to Hugh. She had written: 'Woke up at eight o'clock. Had breakfast. Mrs Green's cat, Smokey climbed a tree. Mr Collins posted a letter. Had lunch. Read a story. A green van called at Mrs Pine's house. Two men took some furniture away in it. Took medicine. Had tea.'

'It's not very exciting, is it Hugh?' she said. I took the van's number, too. But I suppose that's not interesting either.

'Well,' said Hugh, 'something more exciting might happen tomorrow.'

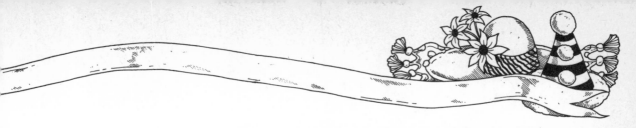

The next day while Debbie lay in bed, a knock came on the front door. Debbie could hear voices downstairs. One of the voices sounded like that of their neighbour Mrs Pine. She could hear Mrs Pine talking. 'They took the television and a radio and some silver. Imagine, we had only been away for two days . . .'

'Mummy,' Debbie called in excitement.

'Wait a moment Debbie,' her mother called back.' Mrs Pine is here. I'll be up to you in a minute.'

'But it's about Mrs Pine,' shouted Debbie, and she jumped out of bed. Her mother and Mrs Pine came upstairs.

'Get back into bed this minute,' said her mother.

'But look. It's all in my diary,' said Debbie.

'What is?' asked Mrs Pine in a puzzled voice.

Debbie started to explain. 'You said that things had been taken from your house. I kept a diary yesterday, and here's the number of the van that was parked outside your gate. I wrote it down. Look!'

'What a clever girl,' said Mrs Pine. 'I'll phone the police and tell them.' And she ran downstairs.

Debbie settled herself comfortably back against the pillows, picked up her diary again, and began to write.

Hide-and-seek

Ever since Sidney Slug had got ten out of ten for a spelling test
at school, he was for ever telling Basil Beetle how brainy he
was. 'I can beat you at anything,' he would boast.

'Okay,' said Basil, who was actually much brainier than
Sidney. 'Let's play hide-and-seek.'

'Right-ho,' said Sidney. 'That's easy. I'll hide first and I bet
you never find me.'

So, while Basil stood behind a flower pot with his eyes
closed counting to fifty, Sidney slid off across the garden to
where he thought was the perfect hiding place – underneath
the watering can beside the greenhouse. He slithered
underneath and waited.

'Coming,' Basil shouted.

Sidney chuckled under the watering can. 'He'll never find
me,' he thought.

But, to Sidney's fury, in no time at all he heard Basil say,
'You're under the watering can, Sidney.'

Sidney crawled out. 'You must have cheated and looked,' he
said crossly. 'How could you have found me so quickly
otherwise?' But Basil just gave a knowing wink and crawled
away.

Can *you* think how Basil found Sidney so quickly? Slugs
leave a silvery trail wherever they go, so Basil just followed the
trail!

Kidnap!

Gertrude Goat was feeling very happy as she trotted along by the side of her friend Gregory. Her two little kids were in the meadow playing together quite safely. At least that's what Gertrude thought they were doing.

It so happened that, unknown to Gertrude, two suspicious looking men were opening the gate that led into the meadow.

'There you are Sam, I reckon we can steal those kids easily,' said Sid.

The two kids were very frightened and ran away as fast as they could. But the men ran even faster and soon caught them. The little kids made a loud bleating calling for help.

Gertrude and Gregory were just finishing a tasty morsel when they heard the kids.

'Come on,' said Gregory. 'We haven't a moment to lose.'

Down to the meadow they ran and through the gate. Gregory had a most marvellous pair of horns. He gave Sid and Sam such a big biff and bang that they ran for their lives and haven't been heard of since.

Knucklebones

You will need:
five small pebbles

This game was played by the ancient Greeks hundreds of years ago. Another name for it is Five Stones. The Greeks played it with five matching bones, but you can use small pebbles instead. They should be the same size.

You can do lots of things with them. First put them in the palm of your hand and toss them up in the air. Spread your fingers and catch as many as you can on the back of your hand.

Now try something different. Put four of the pebbles down and keep one in your hand. Throw this one up in the air. Before you catch it, pick up one of the four pebbles with the same hand. Try picking up two of the pebbles next, then three, then four.

Take turns at these tricks with your friend. The more you practise, the easier they will become.

376

Bean toss

You will need:
dried beans
three bowls
a pencil
paper

If you have a large number of players, divide them into two teams. All you use to play the game are a handful of dried beans, three bowls fitting loosely one inside another and a pencil and paper to keep the score.

Put the 'nest' of bowls at one end of a table. Players now stand at the other end and take it in turns to toss beans into the bowls. The smallest bowl counts three points, the middle size bowl counts two points, and the biggest counts one point. You are not allowed to touch the table.

After each player's throw, count the beans in the different bowls and work out his points. Keep count for each team. The team with the highest score wins.

377

The Globs

Globs are great big, green, greedy space monsters. They fly about the universe in green space ships looking for food. Their favourite things to eat are fruit and trees and grass and flowers. And they are very greedy. When they land on a planet they eat absolutely all the fruit and trees and grass and flowers there are. So it is not very nice to have a visit from the Globs!

One day the Globs saw Planet Earth in the distance. 'That looks a likely place,' said the Chief Glob, licking his enormous lips.

So he sent two space ships down to Earth to see if there was any food to be had. All the rest of the Globs waited up in space licking their enormous lips.

At last one of the ships came back, and the Glob-in-charge made her report. 'It's wonderful,' she said. 'We landed in a warm sunny place where there are lots of trees covered in fruit and lots of grass and lots of flowers.'

All the Globs licked their enormous lips and waited impatiently for the second ship to come back. But when it finally arrived the Globs inside were looking very gloomy. 'There's no food on that planet,' they said. 'Everything is

covered in some cold, hard, white stuff. There's no grass and no flowers to be seen and all the trees look dead.'

The Globs couldn't understand it. Was this planet full of food or wasn't it?

The Chief Glob decided to send two more ships down to Earth to see what they could find. So they set off and the first ship was soon back. 'Everything is growing,' reported the Glob-in-charge. 'There is fresh green grass everywhere and soon lots of flowers will be out.'

All the Globs cheered up and waited impatiently for the second ship, licking their enormous lips.

The second ship was soon back – full of cross looking Globs. 'Everything is dying,' they said. 'All the leaves are falling off the trees and the flowers are dead.'

'It must be magic,' said the Chief Glob. 'There must be a powerful magician on that planet. It is not safe for us to land!'

So all the Globs flew away. It's lucky for us that Globs don't understand that it's winter on one side of the Earth while it's summer on the other, and that it's spring in some countries while it's autumn in others!

379

The baby rabbits

'I'm sorry but I don't think I can come out today,' said Bobby Rabbit to his friend Mole. 'I have to look after my baby brothers and sisters while my mother is away.'

'Well, why can't we take them out with us?' said Mole. 'I'll help you to amuse them.'

'Well,' said Bobby doubtfully, 'they're very naughty, but perhaps some lively games will tire them out.'

So with the baby rabbits frisking round them, they set off towards the lake. After a while Mole looked round. 'Bobby,' he said. 'How many should there be?'

'Er . . . let me see, five I think. There's Sandy, Katie, Maggie, Georgie and Jeremy.'

'Well, there's only four here,' said Mole.

'Oh dear! Jeremy's gone. We must find him. Mother will be so worried.'

By now they had reached the lake, and Georgie suddenly cried, 'Look! There he is, floating along on that log. He's waving to us. Isn't he clever?'

'He's not clever at all,' said Bobby. 'He's floating towards the waterfall, and any minute he'll fall off. What shall we do?'

Just then, a small black head appeared above the water. 'Don't worry,' said Sammy Otter. 'I'll get him.' And in a flash he'd reached the log and pushed it to the shore.

'Thank you Sammy,' said Bobby. He turned round to call

the others. 'Oh dear!' he said. 'Katie isn't here now. This is too much. Where can she be?'

By now they'd reached a gardener's shed, and could hear scratching and squeaking coming from inside. 'That's her,' said Bobby. 'Katie, are you there? Come out at once.'

'I can't,' said Katie. 'I've eaten a lot of seeds, and now I'm too fat to get out.'

'Come on everyone, start digging,' Bobby cried. 'We must make a tunnel for her. Katie, you scrape on your side.'

They had nearly finished when they heard someone coming. It was Mr Potts the gardener! The rabbits hid behind the shed as Mr Potts opened the door and went in.

'Oh, so it's you whose been eating my seeds?' they heard him say. And then such a chasing and scuffling went on inside, until Mr Potts shouted, 'Got you,' and then with a cry of pain he yelled, 'Aah . . . it's bitten me!' He dropped Katie, who landed with a bump on the ground.

'Quick Katie, the tunnel's ready,' cried Bobby, and in a moment she was out, and they all bolted down the nearest rabbit hole.

Mother Rabbit was back when they got home. 'Oh, my dear little babies,' she said. 'Have you all been good? Of course, I know you have.'

'I don't suppose she would believe me if I told her what had happened, or she'd say it was my fault for not looking after them properly,' said Bobby. 'Well, they're all back safely. Come along Moley, let's go out by ourselves.'

Bigboots and the giant

No one liked Bigboots the giant. He was always boasting and showing off. He picked up houses and put them down in different places. He blew all the water out of the duck-pond. He uprooted trees and squashed people's gardens.

The king heard about this naughty giant and he decided to teach him a lesson. He summoned Bigboots to the palace.

Bigboots was a bit scared because, deep down, he knew he had been very naughty. But, to his surprise, the king didn't scold him. Instead he asked Bigboots to help him.

'My gardener – Tinytoes the elf – is finding it too difficult to look after all the palace gardens on his own,' the king said. 'So I thought you might like to help him. You can look after the gardens on the west side of the palace, and Tinytoes

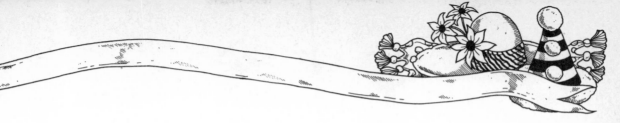

will look after the gardens on the east side.'

Now it was a great honour to be asked to help with the palace gardens. They were famous all over the kingdom.

Bigboots felt sure that he would be a marvellous gardener and he looked at Tinytoes scornfully. 'I shall grow wonderful flowers,' he said boastfully. 'I'm surprised that a tiny elf can do anything at all! I shall be a much better gardener than him.'

The king just smiled to himself and said nothing.

Bigboots started work. He was very good at digging the ground. He was very good at pulling up weeds. He was even quite good at mowing the grass. But he was no good at all at planting seeds, or looking after little tiny plants. His fingers were so big he couldn't hold the seeds! And his feet were so big he trod on all the baby plants!

In the winter Bigboots laughed at Tinytoes trying to clear up the gardens and dig the earth. But when summer came Tinytoes laughed because he had lots and lots of beautiful flowers and Bigboots had none.

When the king came to inspect the gardens one hot summer's day Bigboots hung his head. 'Well,' said the king, 'I hope you have learnt your lesson, Bigboots. You may be good at some things but you are not good at everything. No one is good at everything. Now if you both work together the gardens will be better than ever!'

Kitchen music makers

Saucepan lids make good cymbals.

A saucepan and wooden spoons make a drum.

Make a water xylophone from jam jars or glasses. Fill the jars with different amounts of water. Remember the more water in the glass the lower the note it will produce when you hit it with a spoon.

Two wooden spoons banged together become rhythm sticks.

384

Comb buzzer

YOU WILL NEED
Comb
Tissue paper

Wrap a comb in a piece of tissue paper.
Put it to your lips and blow gently.

Rattle

YOU WILL NEED
Tin or yoghurt pot with a reusable
   lid
Rice or dried peas

Just fill the tin or pot half full with rice
or dried peas and fix the lid on tightly.
Now you have a rattle.

Guitar

YOU WILL NEED
Shallow tin
Elastic bands

Stretch the elastic bands over the tin
and pluck or strum them.

Tooter

Whistle

YOU WILL NEED
Long cardboard tube
Tissue paper
Elastic band

YOU WILL NEED
Sheet of paper
Scissors

1

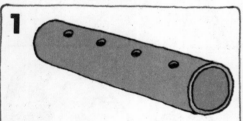

Ask a grown up to punch some holes in the tube.

1

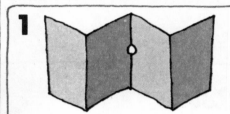

Cut a long strip of paper. Fold it in four and open it out again. Tear a small hole in the centre fold.

2

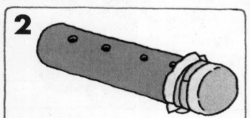

Then cover one end of the tube with tissue paper held in place with an elastic band.

2

3

Blow into the open end.

Hold the whistle to your mouth like this and blow.

386

Foiltop tambourine and shaker

To make a tambourine, thread the bottle tops or circles of foil in groups of three or four and attach them loosely to the edge of the paper plate.

YOU WILL NEED
Paper plate
Stick
Milk bottle tops or small circles of tin foil
Needle and cotton
Sticky tape

To make the shaker thread the foil tops on to lengths of cotton – about 20 tops on each strand. Tie the cotton to the stick. Shake the stick to make a noise.

At the oasis

Nessim was very excited. This was the first time he had been allowed to journey into the great Saudi Arabian desert with his father. But it was very hot and he was glad when they stopped to rest at an oasis where there were palm trees and a pool.

His father nodded off to sleep, and Nessim wandered away into the desert. In the distance, he saw hazy shapes that seemed to shimmer, like reflections in water. They looked like palm trees beside a big lake. Nessim walked towards them. He walked and walked, but they never got any nearer.

It was very, very hot, and he felt dizzy, and sat down. His throat was as dry as dust, and his skin felt as if it was burning. He tried to stand up, but he felt too faint.

Then he heard the voice of his father, who had come to find him. He carried Nessim back to the oasis, and explained that the palm trees and the lake in the distance were not real – they were called a 'mirage', a trick of the light that often happens in deserts.

388

Little bear

Little Bear was wide awake. His mother, brother and sister were all very sleepy for winter was drawing near and bears hibernate in the winter. The days were growing colder and the nights darker and longer.

'Come to bed, Little Bear, said his mother.

But Little Bear took no notice. He went on playing. He jumped, turned somersaults and kept his family wide awake when they wished to sleep.

Then he caught sight of the honey-jar his mother had found in the forest. Mother Bear had brought the jar full of honey home with her, and had told her children, 'We will save this for when we wake up hungry in the spring.'

Little Bear did not want to wait till then, and seeing that his family were nearly asleep, he pulled down the honey-pot, and stuck his nose inside.

Then he found that he could not get it out. 'Owwww-yow-yow,' he yelled. 'Mama, Mama, come and help me.'

Mother Bear, was wide awake by now because of the noise Little Bear was making. She got up and managed to get his nose free of the honey-pot.

'Now go to sleep, you bothersome bear,' she said.

'I'm not tired,' whined Little Bear.

'Yes you are, but you don't know it. Shut your eyes. Tight. Tighter.'

Little Bear screwed up his eyes obediently. He could hear the gentle snores of his brother and sister – they were fast asleep by now.

'Oh well,' thought Little Bear, 'I suppose I am a little bit tired,' and with this last thought, Little Bear fell fast asleep.

The pigeon race

At the bottom of Jackie and Kim's garden, there was a pigeon loft where their dad kept racing pigeons. (Pigeon lofts are special little wooden houses for pigeons.)

One day Jackie and Kim had a big surprise. Their dad gave them two pigeons. 'These two aren't very good at racing,' said Dad, 'but they'll make nice pets. So if you look after them properly – you can have them.'

The pigeons were called Popsy and Mopsy and they had pearly grey and white feathers.

'Fancy Dad saying Popsy and Mopsy aren't good at racing,' said Jackie. 'Let's have a race with them and see. We'll take them to the park in the big shopping basket. Then, we'll let them fly home on their own and we'll ask Mum to let us know which one gets back first.'

So Jackie and Kim took the pigeons to the park. They went right to the middle of a big stretch of grass, and they let Popsy and Mopsy out of the basket. But guess what those two pigeons did?

First they went flying round in circles as if they were playing aeroplanes. Then they went flipping about over the tops of all the trees.

Then they flew close to the pond in the park and landed on the grass right next to where a little girl was feeding some baby ducklings. The two pigeons managed to eat quite a lot

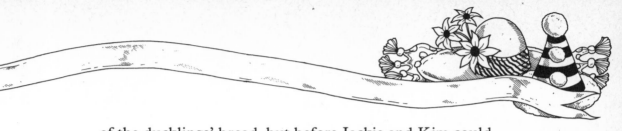

of the ducklings' bread, but before Jackie and Kim could creep up and catch them, they flew up into the air again.

'Perhaps they think the park aviary is a pigeon loft!' said Jackie, as they watched the pigeons walking about on the aviary roof.

'We'll just have to go back home and see if they come back to their loft later on. They don't seem to like racing at all,' said Kim.

When they got back, Dad was down the garden with his proper racing pigeons.

'How are Popsy and Mopsy getting on?' he asked.

'They've got lost in the park,' said Kim. 'I hope someone will see the little rings they are wearing round their ankles and send them back to us.'

Then Mum called from the house. 'Hurry up, tea's ready. I thought you two had got lost in the park.'

'It's Popsy and Mopsy that have got lost, Mum,' said Jackie.

'Popsy and Mopsy?' said Mum. 'They're not lost! They got back ages ago. They're up there on the roof – near the chimney-pot.'

'They must be better at racing than we thought!' said Jackie and Kim.

Hippos and rhinos

There was a great splashing sound as a family of hippos played in the river.

'Come on in, the water's lovely,' they shouted to a lonely little figure who was standing at the water's edge. It was Tiny. He was the only one who didn't like swimming.

'No thanks, it's a bit too deep for me,' he said. But just in case they made fun of him he waded very carefully into the shallowest part, so that the water only came to his ankles.

'Fancy not liking the water,' laughed one of the larger hippos. 'I love it.'

While the big hippo was diving up and down Tiny crept away to find a tasty bush to nibble. This was much nicer, he thought to himself. It was awful when the other hippos pushed him into the water. It would go in his ears and eyes and once he was nearly eaten by a crocodile!

'Hello! What are you up to?' said a voice. Tiny looked round and saw a giraffe.

392

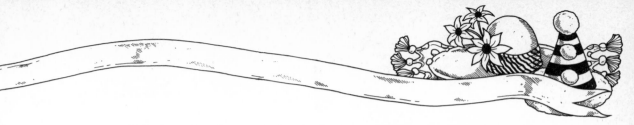

'Oh, just having my elevenses,' he said. As he spoke his nose began to feel itchy. Tiny rubbed it against a tree which made it feel better.

During the next few weeks he began to get a bump where the itchy part had been. All the other hippos made fun of it.

By the time the rainy season had come again Tiny's bump had grown into a lovely point. When he looked at his reflection in the water he could see another bump coming.

He was rather worried about this for none of the other hippos had pointy bits on their noses. So he decided to hide away from them. As he trotted along he saw some other hippos but they were odd just like he was. The smallest one looked friendly.

'Are you going swimming?' asked Tiny.

'No fear,' said the smallest animal. 'I only like water for drinking.'

'Most hippos love swimming,' said Tiny.

'I know, but I'm not a hippo. I'm like you, a rhinoceros.'

So that was it. At last Tiny knew why he hated going into the river. Now he could explain everything to the hippos.

'We are very sorry to have been so unkind to you,' the hippos told him. 'Please forgive us.'

Tiny did forgive them and then he proudly went off to join the other rhinos.

Shell animals

Which animals you make depends on the shells you have, but here are some ideas to get you started. Try and think of some more animals to make yourself.

YOU WILL NEED
An assortment of shells
Strong non-toxic glue
Varnish and brush
Tiny beads for eyes, string for tails
 pipe-cleaners for antennae etc.

When the glue is dry, varnish the shells carefully. This will keep their colours nice and bright.

Shell box

Make sure the lid of the box or tin is clean and dry. Lay the shells on the lid and try out different patterns. When you have found a pattern you like, stick the shells on to the lid. Or if you have some putty you can cover the top of the box with it and stick the shells into that. When the glue or putty is dry, varnish the shells.

A shell box makes a nice present. You can put something inside to make it an extra-special gift.

395

Pebble paperweights

At the seaside and beside some rivers you can find beautiful smooth pebbles. If you paint pictures on these stones they make very pretty ornaments or paperweights.

Always wash the pebbles first and let them dry. If you want, you can draw your design on in pencil first and then paint over it. You can make patterns or pictures. When the paint is dry, cover the stone in a thin layer of varnish.

YOU WILL NEED
Large flat pebbles
Poster paints
Varnish and brush
Pencil

You might find some stones which already look like funny creatures. With some stones, see if you can make a monster!

396

Easy pictures

YOU WILL NEED
Sheets of plain paper
Your paint box, felt pens, crayons or
    wax crayon
Coins

One of the easiest pictures of all to make is a scribble picture. With a crayon scribble all over a sheet of paper. Fill in the scribble in different colours and you will have a very unusual pattern.

Another sort of easy picture to make is a 'draw-round' picture. See if you can create a whole picture just by drawing round a few coins. Have a competition to see who can think of the most unusual things to create using the coins.

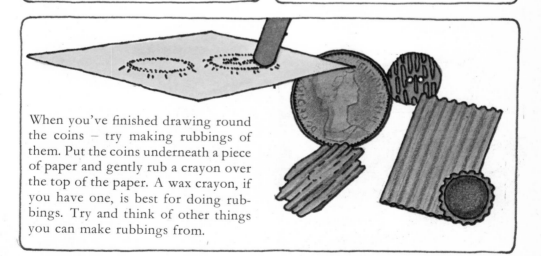

When you've finished drawing round the coins — try making rubbings of them. Put the coins underneath a piece of paper and gently rub a crayon over the top of the paper. A wax crayon, if you have one, is best for doing rubbings. Try and think of other things you can make rubbings from.

Digging a hole

Brian didn't like gardening. Gardening was not fun. It was hard work.

Sometimes, his mother asked him to help with the weeding. Brian liked weeds just as much as flowers. So he wouldn't help. Brian's father asked him to rake up the loose grass after he had cut it. Brian liked the grass long. So he wouldn't help. Brian also liked to see the red, yellow and brown leaves lying all over the garden in autumn. So he wouldn't sweep them up.

One day, his father started to dig a big hole in the front garden. He was going to plant a tree. Brian watched him. After a while, he fetched his beach spade and started to help.

He climbed in the hole, dug his spade into the earth and threw the soil up high on to the edge of the hole.

When the hole was finished, Brian's father lifted him out. Brian looked down. Where there had been solid earth, there was now air. At the edge of the hole, where there had been air, there was now a big pile of earth.

Brian liked digging the hole. It was an important job. And it was fun. He and his father had been playing.

398

Harriet Hare

Harriet Hare had heard a rumour that hares go mad during the month of March.

Which was why, on the first day of March, Harriet Hare woke up and decided she should go mad. 'I don't *feel* mad,' she thought, sitting up in bed. 'But, after all, I am a hare, and all hares go mad in March. I'll just have to pretend to be mad. Otherwise I won't be considered a proper hare.' So she leapt out of bed and did a somersault. Then she slid down the bannister and danced on the kitchen table.

Harriet pretended to be mad all day. She skipped all the way to the shops, and went into the toy shop to buy bread and the greengrocer's to buy pencils. She went into Mrs Squirrel's tea shop, ordered a lime milk shake, and poured it all over her head.

Everyone looked round at her in amazement. 'What *are* you doing, Harriet?' asked Mrs Squirrel.

Harriet grinned. 'It's the first of March today and, because I'm a hare, I've gone mad.'

All the animals in the tea shop roared with laughter. 'Everyone knows that's all nonsense,' said Henry Hedgehog between chuckles.

Harriet did feel silly, sitting there with milk shake running down her ears.

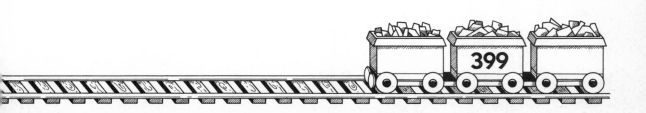

399

Shadows

You will need:
an old sheet
a lamp

Shadows is a game for several players. Divide into two teams.

Ask a grown-up to help you hang an old sheet across the room and put a bright lamp behind it. Turn off the other lights.

To play the game, the members of each team pass between the lamp and the sheet one at a time, and try to disguise themselves with different actions. You can limp, stride, hunch your back, wiggle from side to side or do anything else you like to fool the members of the other team. They are watching from the other side of the sheet and have to guess who the shadows belong to.

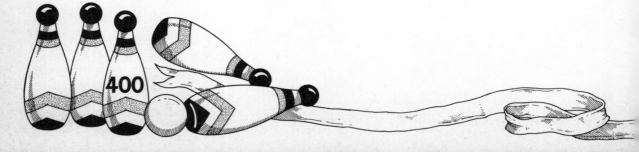

Hidden sentence

You will need:
a pencil
paper

How do you hide a sentence? It is easy. All you have to do is add another letter. Look at what is written below. It doesn't look like a sentence, does it? If you look closer you will see that an extra letter has crept in again and again. See if you can find the hidden letter and make out what the sentence says.

YOBUHABVETOBLOOBKVERBYHABRDTOBFIBNDTHIBSBSE-
NBTENCBE

When you have solved this puzzle, try and make up a sentence of your own. Show it to a friend for her to solve.

The sentence says 'You have to look very hard to find this sentence'. The hidden letter is B.

The cream castle

Franz and Liesl sat in a café, in a little town in Austria, eating Mr Grunwald's delicious cakes. 'You look sad today, Mr Grunwald,' said Liesl. 'What is wrong?'

'I do not have enough customers,' replied the old man. 'Most people go to the big café in the main square for their coffee and cakes. They don't seem to find this little side street. So, I must close my café.'

Sadly Franz and Liesl finished their cakes and went into the main square. A man was nailing a large notice to one of the trees. There was to be a big competition to make a model of Klosberg Castle.

Klosberg Castle stood on a hill outside the town. It was a

402

beautiful castle with lots of round towers and high walls with tiny pointed windows.

'It wouldn't be easy to make a model of the castle,' said Liesl.

Franz agreed. 'But I've an idea. Let's go back and see Mr Grunwald about it.'

On the morning of the competition Franz and Liesl called at Mr Grunwald's little café. 'Is it ready?' they asked.

'I have been working on it all night,' said Mr Grunwald. 'Come and look.'

On the table in the kitchen stood a model of Klosberg Castle. The walls and towers were made of cake and the whole castle was beautifully iced and decorated with cream and chocolate.

'It's wonderful,' said Franz.

'It's like a fairytale castle,' said Liesl. 'You are clever, Mr Grunwald.'

Very carefully they carried the cake up the street to the main square and into the Town Hall. The building was filled with models of Castle Klosberg – in clay, in wood, in stone, in paper, even in matchsticks.

While the judges decided, everyone had to wait outside in the square. At last the Mayor came out and announced, 'The winner is Mr Grunwald with his castle of cake and whipped cream.'

He presented Mr Grunwald with the prize and everyone clapped and cheered before going into the Town Hall to have another look at the wonderful cake castle.

Mr Grunwald was delighted, and when he went home he found a long queue of people waiting outside his café. Everyone wanted to try some of his famous cakes.

Now Mr Grunwald's little café is always busy, but Liesl and Franz know that Mr Grunwald keeps a table in the corner specially for them.

Ladybird, ladybird

Ladybird, ladybird,
Fly away home.
Your house is on fire,
And your children are gone.
All except one,
Whose name is Anne,
And she crept under
The frying pan!

Blow, wind, blow

Blow, wind, blow,
And go, mill, go!
That the miller may grind his corn,
That the baker may take it,
And into bread make it,
And bring us a loaf in the morn.

404

One, two, three, four, five

One, two, three, four, five,
Once I caught a fish alive.
Six, seven, eight, nine, ten,
Then I let it go again.

Why did you let it go?
Because it bit my finger so.
Which finger did it bite?
This little finger on the right.

Tom, Tom, the piper's son

Tom, Tom, the piper's son,
Stole a pig and away did run.
The pig was eat, and Tom was beat,
And Tom went crying down the street.

Oscar's new coat

Oscar was a young snowshoe rabbit who lived in Canada. He
had only been born a few months ago, in spring. Now it was
autumn and he was not looking forward to the cold winter,
which all the older rabbits had told him about. There would
be lots of snow and ice, freezing winds, and for months it
would be dark nearly all the time. He wouldn't be able to
find a nice sunny spot to lie down in and have a short
snooze.

Making his life even more miserable, he had quarrelled
with his best friend, Lucky the lemming. Lucky had laughed
at Oscar because his usually smooth brown coat was falling
out in patches, and white fur was growing instead. Oscar
knew that he looked rather strange, but he could certainly do
without his best friend telling him that. Anyway, Oscar's
mother said it always happened to snowshoe rabbits in
autumn, and next spring, he would get his brown coat back

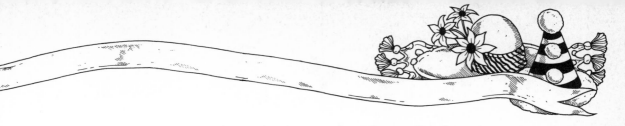

again. Lucky and Oscar had argued, and now Lucky wouldn't speak to him.

Oscar sniffed unhappily at a brownish-green piece of grass made brittle by the frost. He hopped slowly along over the first snow that had fallen, not caring about where he was going. He wished that his feet weren't so cold and that he had his sleek brown fur again.

Suddenly, he heard a loud flapping of wings. It was Sam the snowy owl, looking for a nice young rabbit to make a juicy snack! Oscar stopped absolutely still with fear, hoping that if he didn't move, Sam would not notice him. The owl came nearer and nearer, until a shadow passed over Oscar, and Sam had gone. Oscar was safe!

Just then, a voice squeaked at him from behind a nearby stone.

'I say, Oscar, your new white fur looks very smart now! In fact, if it hadn't been tor your coat hiding you against the snow, old Sam would have been sure to have had you for his supper.'

It was Oscar's friend Lucky, who had also been hiding from the owl. Oscar was pleased that Lucky was speaking to him again. Now he had someone to play with. 'Hullo, Lucky! I tell you what. Why don't I hide, and then you see if you can spot me in my clever new disguise?'

Marble bowls

You will need:
a small cardboard box
some marbles

Here is a different way of using marbles – in a game of bowls.
You can play on your own or with a friend.

Make a scoring box out of a cardboard box. All you have
to do is cut some arches in one side of it. It should also be
open at the bottom. Above the arches write a score number.
Now stand back and roll the marbles through the arches.
Then count your score.

Sticky toffee

This is a tag game. In the simplest sort of tag game, one person chases the others until she touches someone. That person then becomes IT. Sticky Toffee is more complicated. You play it like this.

Choose someone to be IT. Everybody runs off and the IT chases them. As soon as she touches one of them, that player has to join hands with the IT. They now both try to catch the other players. Whoever is touched by one of the ITs must join on to the line. You will soon have a long chain of ITs. The last player to be caught becomes the new IT.

Green apples

All the trees in Mr Plumley's orchard had lots of apples.

'It's a very good year for fruit!' said Mr Plumley happily to himself, as he gathered his crop.

The apple trees were very happy to know that Mr and Mrs Plumley were so pleased with their fruit. Only one tree was sad. She had waited and waited, but Mr Plumley never picked her apples, and she couldn't understand why.

'My apples are big – almost the biggest of all the apples in the orchard,' sighed the sad apple tree. 'Maybe it is because my apples are green, and not red as most of the other apples are. I don't know why my apples haven't turned red. They have had just as much sun as all the other trees. I simply don't understand it all.'

The tree became so sad and droopy that it began to lose its leaves before all the other trees.

Then, one day, right at the end of October, when Mr and Mrs Plumley came into the orchard they came right up to the sad apple tree!

410

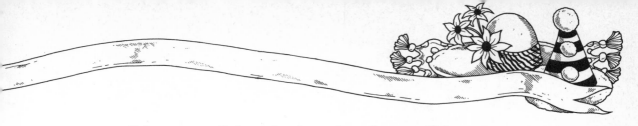

'It's my turn!' thought the sad apple tree. 'It's my turn at last. Mr and Mrs Plumley haven't forgotten about my apples, after all. Now I must listen to what they are saying.'

Mr Plumley said to his wife, 'We'll keep these apples for ourselves. We won't send them to market.'

'Quite right, my dear,' said Mrs Plumley. 'After all, this tree is our only cooking-apple tree.'

'Cooking apples!' said the apple tree to itself. 'So I'm a cooking-apple tree, am I? That's why my apples are so green. They are *meant* to be green.'

How happy the cooking-apple tree was then! She didn't mind about losing her leaves, or about the long winter months ahead. Now she could look forward to next spring when her blossom would appear. After that, she knew her apples would start growing again – her lovely green cooking apples. The cooking-apple tree felt so proud and – never again was she known as a sad apple tree!

Amanda's new dress

Rosemary had a beautiful baby doll. She was called Amanda, and Rosemary played with her every day. The trouble was, Amanda didn't have any clothes. She only wore a nappy, and Rosemary knew that she must be very cold.

Rosemary had a baby sister called Kirsty. She tried one of Kirsty's dresses on Amanda, but it was far too big.

Mummy had promised to make Amanda some clothes, but Rosemary knew that Mummy was very busy and it might be ages before she found the time. Meanwhile, she wrapped Amanda in a blanket to stop her catching cold.

One day, Mummy was taking the washing from the washing machine when she said, 'Oh bother!'

She held up a tiny nightdress and cardigan. 'I am silly,' she said to Rosemary. 'I put Kirsty's clothes in very hot water, and look how they've shrunk.'

Rosemary looked at the tiny clothes and had an idea. 'It doesn't matter,' she said excitedly. 'Now they will fit Amanda.'

After Mummy had dried the nightdress and cardigan, Rosemary tried them on Amanda. They fitted perfectly.

'It's a pity about Kirsty, but she's got lots more clothes,' said Rosemary. 'Now Amanda has got some, too.'

The hula-hula pig

On a small Hawaiian island lived a wild pig called Kokua who wanted, more than anything, to be a hula-hula dancer. Every evening she would hide behind a palm tree and watch the dancers. They wore skirts made of tapa leaves and garlands of flowers, called leis, round their necks.

'How beautiful they look,' thought Kokua. 'And how I wish I could join in.' But no one would ever allow a *pig* to dance!

Then one day Kokua overheard the dancers say that one of the girls was ill and wouldn't be able to dance that evening. It was an important night, too, as lots of tourists were coming to watch.

This was Kokua's chance! She crept to the hut where the dancers kept their costumes, and there hung the spare skirt and garland. She slipped them on. The skirt just fitted round her rather plump waist. After admiring herself in the mirror, she went and joined the dancers on the seashore.

Everyone roared with laughter when they saw Kokua. But when the tourists saw what an excellent dancer she was, they stopped laughing and clapped instead, and they took lots of photographs. What a thing to show the folks back home – a pig hula-hula dancer!

413

The playroom

In Andrew's new house there was a proper playroom. His mother was pleased. 'Now there won't be lots of toys all over the kitchen floor,' she said. She was fussy about the new kitchen.

Andrew didn't like the playroom. He wanted to play in the kitchen, where his mother was. His mother didn't understand. 'You're a lucky boy to have a playroom of your own,' she said.

But Andrew didn't think he was lucky. He felt very lonely, all by himself in the playroom.

One day, when his mother went upstairs, Andrew carried his box of building bricks into the kitchen. He sat on the floor and started to build a house.

He felt happy. It was a busy room. There was something bubbling away on the cooker and he could see the wet clothes and the soapy suds tossing around in the washing machine.

When his mother came downstairs, she wasn't cross at all. She laughed. 'It's nice to see toys on the floor again,' she said. 'I was beginning to feel lonely too, all by myself in the kitchen.'

So Andrew stayed there. He watched his mother cooking, and she watched him building his house. They were both very busy.

414

A picture of Toby

Isabel loved painting. She had a great big paintbox which had lots and lots of colours in it.

One day, she decided to paint a picture of her friend Toby. She painted his nice round cheerful face. She painted his blue jeans and yellow shirt. Then she painted his brown shoes. But when she came to paint his hair, she didn't know what to do.

Toby had thick yellow hair. It was the colour of straw, but Isabel's brother Richard had put a dirty brush in her yellow, and it had turned dark brown. She'd just have to paint Toby with brown hair.

When she'd finished, Isabel looked at her painting. It really didn't look much like Toby.

Mummy came to have a look.

'It doesn't look very like Toby,' said Isabel, disappointed.

'It's not like Toby,' Mummy said, 'but it is like Daddy. He's got hair that colour and he sometimes wears jeans and a yellow shirt.'

Isabel stared at her painting. Mummy was right. It was just like Daddy. She was so pleased, that she pinned it up on the wall, and when Daddy came home he said, 'That looks just like me.'

Isabel and Mummy looked at each other and smiled.

415

Mr Stray

Mr Stray was an old, battered, wheezy stray cat.

Timothy heard him meowing outside the front door one cold rainy day. When he opened it, in walked the old cat.

'That's a real wandering cat, I can tell,' Timothy's father said. 'He won't stay long so let's call him Mr Stray.'

'Yes, give Mr Stray a bowl of milk,' Timothy's mother suggested, 'and then he'll probably wander away again.'

But how wrong they all were! First Mr Stray slept all that day in front of the fire. Then he slept all that night in front of the fire. When he awoke he stretched, yawned and just lay in front of the fire until his next meal.

On and on this went with Mr Stray getting so fat and well-fed, so sleek and so chubby and round they soon had to think of another name for him.

Mother suggested Fatty. Father said they could call him Chubby. But Timothy's name was best.

'Mr Stay!' he said, 'let's call him Mr Stay, because he just stays and stays and stays!'

In fact Mr Stay is staying there still for all we know.